BREAKFAST

morning, noon and night

BREAKFAST
morning, noon and night

FERN GREEN

PHOTOGRAPHY BY DANIELLE WOOD

hardie grant books

MELBOURNE · LONDON

CONTENTS

INTRODUCTION

I love breakfast. I never used to. When I was at school, eating breakfast used to be time wasted when you could be catching a few more Zs in bed. Breakfast was boring: cereal or toast. These seemed like the only two options when you had just 10 minutes to eat before leaving to catch the school bus. Reminded incessantly by my mum that 'breakfast is the most important meal of the day', I simply ignored her advice like a typical teenager.

My brothers and sisters didn't feel the same way. Milk and cereal were consumed at pretty much any time of the day, right up until just before they went to bed. Frosties, Crunchy Nut and Cocoa Pops, even slices of toast with Marmite or chocolate spread; they had these for snacks as well as breakfast.

Unless something prevented him from doing so, my grandad had a boiled egg for breakfast every single morning of his adult life. Quite a phenomenal achievement, considering I can't imagine many people doing that these days.

My own love for breakfast started one weekend in my late teens. When I was old enough to start going out to bars and clubs, I discovered the rejuvenating powers of a fry–up. This love grew at university when I had the use of my own kitchen and started to experiment with what to cook. Feeding my new friends an unusual or creative breakfast morning, noon or night was special and became very important to me.

Since then, I have visited and had breakfast in many different countries, and tasting the vast array of flavours available continued to widen its appeal to me. My love for breakfast was confirmed.

Breakfast is personal. Everybody has their favourite, although I have found that there are some common popular breakfasts from doing my own research. I have also found that breakfast is a comforting meal, especially when eaten alone. A meal that only you know how to make, and that way is the best way. You like your porridge your way, you toast your bread the way you like it. You know how to make your favourite cuppa. These are all individual ways of creating the ultimate breakfast, ways that have been developed from your childhood. Or perhaps you started late like me.

Breakfast is the first meal you eat after you wake up: breaking the fast after you have slept. But this meal has broken many a time barrier; as I experienced in my own family when I was younger, breakfast isn't just for the morning. Breakfast is now eaten at any time of the day. Bars, pubs and cafés all serve breakfast around the clock, you can have it whenever you fancy it. As well as inviting our friends round for dinner, we now also invite them round for brunch. Bloody Marys, hot croissants, omelettes and a bacon hash – fancy coming over? The brunch scene is booming, and breakfasts are where it's at.

The collection of recipes in this book are to be eaten whenever you want to eat them. There are so many favourite breakfasts, and too many to fit in here. From my experience of working as a chef across Europe, I have tried to give you a wide spread of flavours, and hopefully many surprising and delicious dishes that you can either share with your friends or just enjoy by yourself.

THE EGG

The egg is a vital ingredient in any breakfast, and one that often takes centre stage – and rightly so.

THE IMPORTANCE OF FRESHNESS

You may have experienced a bad egg once in your lifetime. But to continually experience really good eggs, you need to understand how important a fresh egg is. There is nothing like picking a warm egg straight from a chicken pen, poaching it in some boiling water and eating it on buttered toast. I don't add vinegar to the water when poaching an egg this fresh, there's no need as the egg whites hold together naturally and don't disperse.

Fresh eggs have only a small air pocket inside the shell and as an egg gets older, the air pocket becomes bigger. Therefore, the bigger the air pocket, the older the egg and the more the egg will float when immersed in water. A really fresh egg sinks to the bottom of the water and almost lies on its side. An egg that sinks to the bottom but tilts up slightly (the air pocket has grown), is up to a week old. If it floats in a vertical position, you've got yourself a relatively stale egg but it's still edible. If the egg floats completely, then plop it in the bin.

I recommend eating eggs within two weeks of laying. Make friends with someone who has chickens, or get to know a local farm shop. This is how you can be sure of knowing the freshness of your eggs.

CRACKING IT

Are you a one-hander, or is there a certain surface in your kitchen that you like to crack your eggs on? Perhaps you have a gadget or just simply use the side of the bowl. Cracking eggs can go wrong quite easily. Try quail eggs; they are fiddly little things, but worth it when you have mastered how to crack them. Pierce the shell with a small, sharp knife and gently saw a little line horizontally across it, about 1 cm (½ in) long. You can now pull the shell apart with your fingernails. If you don't have any fingernails, then keep sawing until you can get your fingertips in to break the shell.

To help prevent the yolk from breaking, crack the egg into a small cup or bowl (I use an espresso cup) first. Ta da!

ULTIMATE GUIDE TO POACHING IN NUMBERS

This is a foolproof way of poaching eggs, especially for more than four people – you can even take it up to 16 if you have two large frying pans!

Using a large frying pan, fill it with water up to 2 cm deep, this will barely cover the top of the egg but this is what you want. Now bring the water up to a gentle simmer and add a tablespoon of white wine vinegar. This helps the eggs stay together. Crack your eggs into the simmering water one at a time or use a cup and bring the water back up to a boil. Once the water is boiling leave your eggs to cook for

one more minute then turn the heat down to a simmer and cook for a further 3 minutes. If the eggs look a little raw on top, splash a little bit of the hot water over using a spoon. The best bit now is that you can keep these eggs resting in the water for a good 3–4 minutes to keep warm whilst you prep your toast.

As for lifting them out the pan, use a spatula with holes, this helps drain the liquid away. An alternative to make sure you never have soggy toast is to put your egg on some kitchen paper first before then picking up to place it on top of you toast. Enjoy serving perfect poached eggs.

HOW TO BOIL THE PERFECT EGG

To make the perfect soft–boiled egg, fill a saucepan with enough water to completely submerge the egg. Add a pinch of salt (mainly for precaution; if your egg cracks, it will help keep the white inside the shell). Bring the water to the boil, then turn it down to a simmer. Before you lower in the egg, warm the shell in the steam for a few seconds. Depending on how soft or hard you want your egg, cook it for between 4–7 minutes:

4 minutes yolk very runny; white a bit runny too

5 minutes yolk runny; white just a little runny

6 minutes yolk creamy with firm tinge; white firm

7 minutes yolk and white both firm

THE FINAL BAKE OFF

There are lots of myths about cooking eggs and how to store them, but one rule of thumb is never bake with a cold egg. They encourage splitting and need to be bought up to room temperature if they have been stored in the fridge.

I don't put my eggs in the fridge. For one, I can't stand that eggy holey thing in fridge door. The space is much better used for even more condiments! And two, eggs are not around long enough in my kitchen to even think about wanting to make them last any longer. However, if you do put your eggs in the fridge, make sure you warm them up again by sitting on them for at least 5 minutes. Just kidding. Take them out of the fridge an hour before you start to bake.

Please note that I use large, free-range eggs in my recipes unless otherwise specified; free-range eggs are always deliciously tasty and are kind to the hen.

BREAKFAST UTENSILS

If you are into your gadgets, then you might be aware of the eclectic mix of breakfast paraphernalia that is out there on the market today. When I came to write this part of the book, I had a lovely little list of what I thought were essential utensils for making breakfasts.

I had the **spatula**: the round one with the holes in, and also the square one, which is good for flipping.

I had the **large palette knife**: again useful for flipping, but flipping pancakes especially.

The **espresso cup**: necessary for breaking eggs into.

The **small frying pan**, the **large frying pan**, the **flat hotplate** and the **griddle pan**. All very useful for frying and poaching eggs, to make omelettes, pancakes and even producing fabulous waffles.

Tongs. Useful for turning bread over if grilling. Helpful for turning sausages and bacon too.

The **egg cup**. A vessel used to put your boiled egg in to have with your soldiers.

A decent **deep muffin tray**.

A **whisk**, to whisk your eggs.

An **egg timer**.

I then remembered a random wedding present, which, I must admit, has never been used. Two metal hearts, which you can put in a frying pan to poach your eggs in. I'm not one for Valentine's Day specials, but if you are, then perhaps this is something you can use to make your dear loved one a heart-shaped egg!

This then led me to the internet to see if there were any other funny gadgets that one might use – or more likely, never use! I've kept it to a minimum of three.

Ceramic bacon cooker. A ceramic mug with a built-in fat catcher at the bottom, which you hang bacon on then put in the microwave to cook it. Now why didn't that take off?!

The **pancake pen**. A plastic bottle that holds your pancake batter, with a small hole at one end. You squirt out your mix into fun patterns or the letters of your name!

A **toast stamper**. Exactly what it sounds like, a stamp in many different guises that you stamp on your toast to make a pattern.

Most cooking utensils are useful, breakfast gadgets like these, however, are not.

Comforting. Easy. Eaten at any time of the day.
Fast. Crunchy. Toast is simply the best! Whether you char it
on a griddle, drop it in a toaster, or put it under the grill, we
all know how to make our toast taste the best. The following
recipes include a variety of breads and offer different
ways to make toast to get the most out of it.

ON TOAST

WILD MUSHROOMS & EGGS

SERVES 2

2 thick slices seeded bread

1 garlic clove, peeled

4 tablespoons olive oil

1 sprig thyme

400 g (14 oz) mixed wild mushrooms

salt and freshly ground black pepper

1 tablespoon chopped flat-leaf parsley

2 tablespoons butter

2 eggs

You need a good seeded type of bread when making this, to give it a lovely bit of crunch. The mushroom selection is up to you, though I like using portobellos for their meatiness. See what is in season and give it a go.

Preheat the oven to 140°C (275°F/Gas 1). Toast the bread in a hot griddle pan for about 2–3 minutes on each side, so you get those tasty charred lines. Rub one side of the toasts with the garlic. then drizzle 1 tablespoon of olive oil over each slice and sprinkle with thyme. Keep the toast in the warm oven.

Heat the remaining olive oil in a frying pan over a medium heat, then add the mushrooms. Season and sauté until golden brown, about 4–5 minutes. Add the parsley, stir, then transfer into a bowl. Wipe the frying pan with kitchen towel (kitchen paper) and add the butter. Fry the eggs in the melted butter until the whites are cooked through and the yolks are cooked to your liking – I prefer them soft.

Transfer the toast from the oven to a plate, top with the mushrooms and finish with the fried egg on top. Season to taste and serve.

SPANISH TOMATO TOAST

SERVES 2

2 large or 4 small ripe
tomatoes (cherry tomatoes
won't work here)
pinch of salt
glug of extra virgin olive oil
4 slices sourdough bread

You must have very ripe tomatoes and good quality olive oil to make this dish work. Hardly any other flavours are added apart from the slightly charred toast, which is a must. Found in cafés across Spain, this simple breakfast has the potential to become a new favourite – especially in the summer months.

Using a big box grater, or something similar, carefully grate the juicy tomatoes into a bowl. Grate until you can't grate any more, avoiding knuckle scrapes.

Add a pinch of salt and a good glug of olive oil, and mix together to make a tomato 'nectar'. Let the flavours combine for 5 minutes while you char the bread.

Get a griddle pan nice and hot over a high heat, then char the bread for 2–3 minutes on each side. When all the bread is toasted, take it to the table along with your tomato nectar and spoon some over your toast. Sunshine on toast!

AVOCADO ON TOAST

SERVES 2

1 avocado
1 lime
4 slices sourdough bread
large pinch of salt
pinch of paprika

This breakfast is ever so simple, yet ever so delicious. It's the breakfast I eat when alone, or my lunch when I feel like something quick and tasty. I like to sprinkle a pinch of paprika over it in the morning, but if I am eating it for lunch I sometimes pour over sesame oil and soy sauce and slice up a few chillies. Sourdough is great with it, but any toasted flat bread or pitta is rather good too.

Slice the avocado in half and remove the stone. Using a dessertspoon, scoop the flesh out of each half and put it in a bowl. Squeeze over the juice from the lime and mash together with the back of a fork. I like to keep the avocado a little chunky so that it has some bite. Once you are happy with the texture, toast your sourdough. I like to do this on the hob so you get a few charred parts for a smoky taste. Once toasted, pop the sourdough on to a plate, then spread with the avocado, sprinkle with salt and paprika, and take a large mouthful.

FRENCH TOAST THREE WAYS

SERVES 4

4 eggs
salt and freshly ground
black pepper
4 thick slices white bread
(preferably a stale bloomer)
butter for frying

This is my husband's favourite, which he likes to refer to as 'eggy bread'. French toast is his breakfast speciality and a dish that he ate with his brothers for most of their growing-up years. His recipe is the basis for all three versions here, as I feel it is well tested and trusted, and I'm on a promise!

Preheat the oven to 140°C (275°F/Gas 1) and place a baking tray inside. Beat the eggs in a shallow bowl wide enough to lay the bread flat in and season with salt and a good grinding of pepper. Put a slice of bread in the bowl and allow the bread to absorb the egg for 30 seconds on each side. Meanwhile, melt a large knob of butter in a medium frying pan and add the first slice of soaked bread. Allow to cook undisturbed for 2 minutes, as this lets the egg set properly, giving it a nice crispy texture on the outside. Cook until golden and crisp. Flip the bread over and cook for 1 minute on the other side. Transfer to the warmed baking tray and keep in the oven until you have cooked all 4 slices.

SIMPLY TOMATOES

My husband loves this topping and it's one that I never tire of. Thickly slice **a large tomato** and grill or fry it with loads of seasoning. To enhance the savouriness, you can add some **thinly sliced spring onions (scallions)** on top of the egg-soaked bread as you are frying it.

MAPLE BUTTER & RED SUMMER FRUITS

To make the maple butter, add to a large bowl **110 g (3¾ oz) softened butter, 50 ml (2 fl oz) maple syrup** and **half a teaspoon of almond extract**. Using a fork, mix well, add **a pinch of salt** and mix again. Once all combined, scrape the mixture into a small serving bowl or butter dish and use within the hour, or refrigerate until needed if making this in advance. Slice **strawberries** into a bowl, add some **raspberries** and **redcurrants** and serve the fruit on the side along with the bowl of maple butter so that people can add what they want to their French toast.

BLUEBERRY & BANANA SANDWICHES

Instead of using white bread to make the French toast, cut **a brioche loaf** into 8 slices. Make the egg mixture but add **100 ml (3½ fl oz) milk** and **a pinch of cinnamon**. Halve **2 bananas** and cut each piece in half again lengthways, so you have 8 long slices of banana. Lay 4 slices of brioche inside a small baking dish and arrange the banana on top. Scatter over **100 g (3½ oz) blueberries**, drizzle with **4 tablespoons of clear honey** and then top with the remaining slices of brioche. Pour the egg mixture into the dish and let the sandwiches soak it up for 5 minutes. Turn the sandwiches over and let them soak for 5 minutes on the other side. Keep turning and soaking until all the mixture has been absorbed. Fry the sandwiches in **butter** for 3–4 minutes each side until golden brown. Transfer to plates and dust with **1 tablespoon of icing sugar**.

GOAT'S CHEESE & CHIVES SCRAMBLE
on Seeded Wholegrain

SERVES 2

4 eggs

salt and black pepper

10 g (½ oz) butter, plus extra for buttering the toast

120 g (4 oz) soft goat's cheese

1 tablespoon snipped fresh chives

2 slices seeded wholegrain bread

This lovely soft scramble on toast is extremely comforting and often made when we have guests as an alternative breakfast. I also quite happily eat this for lunch on a summer's day with a watercress salad.

Lightly beat the eggs in a bowl with a dash of water to loosen the mixture. Season to your liking; I like to season generously.

Melt the butter in a frying pan, add the beaten eggs and turn the heat down to low. This helps the scramble stay silky. When the eggs start to solidify, crumble in the goat's cheese and stir intermittently. Take the scramble off the heat when it is almost cooked through; it should still look creamy and not too solid. Add the chives and stir to combine. Toast and butter the bread, and top with a large spoonful of scramble. Lovely served with some tomato chutney.

HOME-MADE CRUMPETS

SERVES 4

180 ml (6½ fl oz) whole milk

120 ml (4 fl oz) boiling water

1 teaspoon caster (superfine) sugar

1 tablespoon fast-action dried yeast

170 g (6 oz/generous 1⅓ cups) strong white flour

80 g (3 oz/scant ⅔ cup) plain (all-purpose) flour

1 teaspoon salt

50 ml (2 fl oz) warm water

½ teaspoon bicarbonate of soda

20 g (¾ oz) unsalted butter

Crumpets are a bit more special than your everyday toast and can be used instead of toast in any of the recipes in this chapter. Alternatively, serve with lashings of butter and any type of jam; making your own crumpet is well worth it.

In a bowl, mix together the milk, boiling water and sugar, and then stir in the yeast – do not add the yeast directly to the boiling water as the high temperature will kill it and your crumpets won't rise. Set aside.

Combine the flours and salt in a large mixing bowl. When the yeast mixture is frothy (this takes about 10 minutes) pour it into the flour. Stir well until the batter is smooth. Cover the bowl with a damp cloth or tea towel (kitchen towel) and leave for around 2 hours, until the batter is showing tiny bubbles.

Mix the warm water with the bicarbonate of soda and pour into the batter. This will help create a really bubbly looking crumpet.

Use 4 crumpet rings and brush the insides with softened butter. Add a little butter to a frying pan over a medium heat and put your rings in the pan. Ladle the batter into the rings until they are half full.

Fry the crumpets until their tops are dry and covered in little holes. Run a knife around the edges of the crumpets and carefully release them from the rings. If you would like to eat them straight away, grill them until golden. Divine when smothered only with butter.

DEVILLED KIDNEYS ON TOAST

SERVES 1

3 lamb's kidneys (veal kidneys are lovely too)

½ teaspoon hot paprika

pinch of cayenne pepper

dash of hot pepper sauce (Marcus likes Tabasco)

1 teaspoon Dijon mustard

½ teaspoon wholegrain mustard

1 teaspoon Worcestershire sauce

1 tablespoon tomato ketchup

1 tablespoon olive oil

salt

1 tablespoon Madeira

2 tablespoons double (heavy) cream

handful of chopped parsley

1 thick slice bread, toasted (a bloomer works well)

My brother Marcus cooks this dish when he feels he needs some nourishment – it's definitely for a 'real man', as he would say! I would say it is for someone who likes big, gutsy flavours and can take a bit of heat with the offal.

Remove the outer membrane from the kidneys and slice them in half lengthways. Using a sharp pair of scissors or knife, cut out their white cores. In a large bowl, mix together the paprika, cayenne, hot pepper sauce, both mustards, Worcestershire sauce and ketchup. Add the kidneys and toss to coat, then leave them to marinate for at least 15 minutes and for up to 4 hours if possible – the longer the better.

Heat a frying pan and add the olive oil. Make sure the pan is very hot, then add the kidneys along with the marinade. Season and cook for 2–3 minutes on each side until just cooked through. Add the Madeira and cook for 20 seconds, then add the cream and boil for another 30 seconds or so.

Stir in the parsley and serve on toast.

LUXURIOUS CHEESE ON TOAST

SERVES 4

70 g (2½ oz) butter

3 tablespoons plain (all-purpose) flour

500 ml (17 fl oz) whole milk

8 rashers (slices) smoked pancetta

50 g (2 oz) hard mozzarella, grated

150 g (5 oz) mature Cheddar, grated

salt and freshly ground black pepper

4 thick slices granary bread

2 tablespoons Dijon mustard

tomato ketchup to taste

1 tablespoon finely chopped parsley to serve

This is my all-time favourite 'on toast' light meal or weekend breakfast. I used to have competitions with my brother to see who could make the best ever cheese on toast. This is my winning version after making some slight alterations through the years.

First make a white sauce by melting 50 g (2 oz) of the butter in a saucepan over a medium heat. Mix in the flour and cook for 3 minutes, stirring occasionally to prevent the roux from sticking to the pan. Slowing whisk in the milk and bring to a simmer, then stir constantly for 5 minutes until you have a smooth, thick sauce. If it goes a bit lumpy use your whisk to stir it until the lumps disappear.

Meanwhile, cook the pancetta under a hot grill for around 2 minutes each side until it is nice and crispy. Remove from the grill when done and set aside, but keep the grill on.

Add both cheeses to the sauce, season with salt and pepper, and stir to combine. Once the cheese has melted, put the bread under the hot grill. It is important that you toast your bread on one side before you add the cheese. I feel this is a vital step: if you forget, you'll be left with a wobbly bit of bread that doesn't stand up to the gooey cheese. Disappointing.

When toasted on one side, remove from the grill and turn the slices over. Spread half a tablespoon of mustard on to each slice, then squirt on some ketchup and spread it over the mustard. Lay 2 rashers of pancetta on top of each piece and then spoon over the cheese sauce. Return to the grill and cook until golden and bubbling.

Serve up your luxurious cheese on toast with a sprinkling of parsley.

SPICED PLUMS
with Yoghurt on Toasted Brioche

SERVES 4

FOR THE HOME-MADE YOGHURT

2.25 litres whole milk (for extra creamy), semi-skimmed will work too

140 ml (4¾ fl oz) yoghurt, Greek yoghurt is great, but any natural yoghurt is good. Check that it contains 'live active yoghurt cultures' on the back as this is what you need to make more yoghurt.

FOR THE PLUMS

500 g (1 lb 2 oz) ripe plums

60 ml (2 fl oz) honey

2 tablespoons maple syrup

½ stick cinnamon

1 star anise

1 teaspoon balsamic vinegar

200 ml (7 fl oz) water

4 thick slices brioche

Brioche is a lovely soft, sweet bread, full of butter and eggs. I've paired it here with some fragrant, warm plums and a delightful cool, homemade yoghurt.

Firstly make your yoghurt as this is best done the day before you want to eat it. You can double the ingredients if you wish to make a bigger batch to keep in the fridge.

Now heat the milk in a saucepan to about 95°C (200°F). Stir the milk gently making sure the bottom doesn't burn or it doesn't boil over. Cool until it is just about warm to touch, roughly 46°C (115°F). Stir occasionally to prevent skin forming. If skin does form, just pull it out or stir it back in.

Add 200ml (7 fl oz) to the yoghurt and gently stir it through using a whisk. When combined, stir the yoghurt mixture into the warm milk whisking as you go. Now wrap the pot in towels and put it in a warm place to set. My mum recommended using a thermos flask which works a treat.

Leave for at least 4 hours or even better, overnight. The longer you leave it the thicker it gets and the more tart it tastes. Perhaps test yours after 4 hours to see if it is how you like it.

Once set, remove the watery whey from the surface and transfer into a storage container. This can be stored in the fridge for up to 2 weeks. Save 140 g (4¾ oz) to make your next batch.

Now for your plums; I find that baking the plums keeps them more intact than poaching them. Preheat the oven to 160°C (320°F/Gas 3). Stone and halve the plums, then put them in a baking dish, cut side down, in a nice snug fit. Put the remaining ingredients for the plums into a saucepan and bring to the boil. Once boiling and the mixture feels a little syrupy, remove the cinnamon stick and star anise and pour over the plums. Cover with foil and place in the oven for 25–30 minutes.

Toast the brioche slices and serve on a plate alongside your home-made yoghurt and a large spoonful of soft, spicy plums.

Eating something that you know is good for you, whether it be in the morning or later in the day, can give you a satisfying sense of superiority. Get to know some of the recipes in this section and you will start to feel rather good about yourself. Then share them with people you love. That feels even better.

HEALTHY

NUTTY, SEEDY, FRUITY GRANOLA

MAKES 1.2 KG (2 LB 10 OZ)

900 g (2 lb) rolled oats

100 g (3½ oz) sesame seeds, white or black, or both

100 g (3½ oz) chopped walnuts

50 g (2 oz) ground or milled flaxseeds

2 tablespoons chia seeds (available online or in most health food shops)

1 teaspoon ground cinnamon

½ teaspoon salt

100 ml (3½ fl oz) honey or maple syrup

100 ml (3½ fl oz) olive oil (not extra virgin as this is too flavoursome)

100 g (3½ oz) mixed dried fruit (if you are using dates reduce the amount of honey to taste)

There is nothing like having your own home-made granola stored in a large airtight jar to grab any time you feel like pouring out some crunchiness and pairing it with some delicious home-made yoghurt. You can use any combination of dried fruit you wish, while coconut is also a great addition.

Preheat the oven to 180°C (350°F/Gas 4). Thoroughly combine all the ingredients except the dried fruit in a large bowl. Spread the mixture out on a baking tray and bake for 20–25 minutes until golden brown and fragrant; give the granola a good stir halfway through cooking. Remove from the oven and leave it to cool.

Add the dried fruit and enjoy with a dollop of home-made yoghurt (see page 30).

BIRCHER MUESLI

SERVES 4

200 g (7 oz) rolled oats

400 ml (14 fl oz) apple juice
or almond milk
(any milk will work)

1 large apple

1 tablespoon raisins

100 g (3½ oz) plain yoghurt
(home-made yoghurt brings
it to a new level, see page 30)

1 tablespoon honey

1 teaspoon cinnamon

When we serve up a buffet-style breakfast for guests, this dish always gets completely demolished. I always hope there is some left over for us, but I find myself making more every time. I do play around with the ingredients, depending on what I have in the cupboard, but this version is tried and tested and keeps you full all morning.

Add to a big bowl the oats and apple juice or milk. For a better flavour and texture, leave the oats soaking overnight or for at least a few hours.

Grate the apple, skin included, into the bowl with the soaked oats. Add the raisins and yoghurt, and give it a good stir. If you find the texture a bit stiff, just add a little more yoghurt to loosen. Squeeze or drizzle over the honey and sprinkle with cinnamon.

PORRIDGE
with Pine Nut Milk

SERVES 4

FOR THE PINE NUT MILK

100 g (3½ oz) pine nuts

350 ml (12 fl oz) water

½ teaspoon vanilla extract (optional)

FOR THE PORRIDGE

100 g (3½ oz) porridge oats

100 ml (3½ fl oz) pine nut milk

There is something unique about the flavour of toasted pine nuts, and when they are made into a milk this flavour is enhanced, while giving the milk a sumptuous creamy taste. Delicious with porridge oats, for a luxurious twist on a staple winter breakfast.

To make the pine nut milk, dry fry the pine nuts in a large frying pan over a medium heat for 3–5 minutes until they are golden and toasted; be sure to stir or shake the pan frequently so the nuts don't burn and they are toasted on all sides. Once cool, transfer the nuts to a bowl, cover with cold water and soak for 4 hours.

Drain the pine nuts and put them into a food processor. Add the water and vanilla extract (if using). Blend for 1 minute. Using a fine sieve, drain the milk into a bowl or jug and discard the pulp from the sieve. The milk can be stored covered in your fridge for up to 3 days.

For the porridge, put the oats and pine nut milk into a saucepan over a medium heat. Stir until it comes up to the boil, then turn the heat right down. Let it simmer until you get your preferred porridge consistency. I like mine slightly runny, which takes about 6–7 minutes. If you want to add some fruit, bananas, apples or peaches go rather well with the pine nut flavour.

INDIAN LENTIL CRÊPE
with Coconut Chutney

FOR THE CHUTNEY

225 g (8 oz) freshly grated coconut

2 small green chillies, chopped (optional)

1 teaspoon freshly grated ginger

1 tablespoon roasted chana dal

1 teaspoon oil

½ teaspoon yellow mustard seeds

1 red chilli, chopped in 3 pieces (optional)

2–3 fresh or dried curry leaves

salt to taste

FOR THE CRÊPES

45 g (1½ oz/scant ¼ cup) basmati rice

45 g (1½ oz) toor dal

45 g (1½ oz) chana dal

45 g (1½ oz) green mung beans

½ small onion

6 fresh or dried curry leaves

pinch of asafoetida

1 cm (½ inch) piece ginger, peeled

1 spring onion (scallion)

3 sprigs coriander (cilantro)

15–20 black peppercorns

½ teaspoon fenugreek seeds

225 ml (8 fl oz) water

1 green chilli (optional)

coconut oil or olive oil for frying

If you fancy something healthy and spicy, these crêpes might be just what you are looking for. Made with lentils, they are gluten free and have a fantastic taste which makes you feel somewhat exotic.

To make the chutney, put the coconut, green chillies (if using), ginger and chana dal into a food processor and blend to a fine paste. You can also use a pestle and mortar for this. Heat the oil in a small frying pan over a medium heat and add the mustard seeds, red chilli (if using) and curry leaves, and stir until the mustard seeds start to pop. Transfer to a bowl, add the coconut mixture and mix well. Season with salt to your taste. You can store this chutney in a sterilised jar in the fridge for up to a month – just make sure it is covered or your jar has a lid.

For the crêpes, soak the rice, dals and mung beans in water for 1 hour. Put all the crêpe ingredients, apart from the oil, into a food processor and blend until the mixture is smooth – similar to a pancake batter consistency. You can keep the mixture in the fridge, covered, for up to 3 days if you would like to make it ahead of time.

Preheat the oven to 140°C (275°F/Gas 1). Heat up a skillet or heavy-based frying pan and add 1 teaspoon of coconut or olive oil. Quickly wipe the oil around the pan with kitchen towel (kitchen paper) to coat the base. (You could also use an oil spray if you have one; I find sprays are quite useful for oiling pans and muffin tins, etc.) Ladle or spoon some batter into the centre of the pan and create a thin crêpe by rolling the pan in a circular motion so the mixture covers its base to the edges of the pan. Fry for 3–4 minutes until it is golden brown. Flip the crêpe over carefully using a spatula and cook for a further 1½ minutes. Slide the crêpe from the pan on to a plate and, when cool enough to handle, quickly roll it up. Transfer the rolled crêpe to an oven-proof dish and put in the oven to keep warm while you make the rest of the crêpes with the remaining mixture. Serve with the delicious coconut chutney.

CHIA SEED, COCONUT & DATE BREAKFAST BOWL

SERVES 1

2 tablespoons chia seeds
(available online or in most
health food shops)

180 ml (6½ fl oz) almond milk
(or any milk)

2 tablespoons desiccated
coconut

3 dried pitted dates, chopped

½ mango, sliced (optional)

yoghurt to serve

whole skin–on almonds,
chopped to serve

Don't be frightened by the frogspawn appearance that chia seeds can create when added to liquid. They are extremely good for you – high in omega–3, fibre, calcium, zinc and iron – and give this dish a lovely, perky crunch. Chia seeds help boost energy, stabilise your blood sugar, aid in digestion and lower cholesterol. An almost essential weekly breakfast bowl.

Like the Bircher muesli (page 35), this recipe works best if you soak the ingredients overnight or for at least 2–3 hours.

Combine the chia seeds, milk, coconut and dates in a bowl, and leave in the fridge overnight or for at least 2–3 hours.

Remove the bowl from the fridge and give it a good stir; it probably will have separated so this brings it all together. Spoon into your breakfast bowl, add the mango (you can substitute this for any other stone fruit), a dollop of yoghurt and sprinkling of almonds.

EGG & BACON UDON

2 tablespoons sesame oil,
plus extra to serve

1 thumbnail-size piece of
ginger, peeled and sliced

2 garlic cloves, peeled and
lightly crushed

2 teaspoons soy sauce

2 teaspoons fish sauce

1 dried kaffir lime leaf

1 litre (1 pint 14 fl oz)
chicken stock

1 teaspoon sesame seeds

2 chestnut mushrooms,
sliced

85 g (3 oz) udon noodles,
uncooked

1 tablespoon white wine
vinegar for poaching
the eggs

2 eggs

2 rashers (slices) bacon

2 tablespoons roughly
chopped coriander (cilantro)

handful of spinach

1 tablespoon chilli oil

pinch of shichimi togarashi
(optional)

In the colder months, a warm broth with some of my favourite breakfast flavours is just what is necessary. This Japanese-style broth is tasty served with a drizzle of chilli oil and extra sesame oil. Sometimes I add a little bit of shichimi togarashi, which is a Japanese seven-spice mix made up of sichuan pepper, dried citrus peel, sesame seeds, poppy seeds, hemp seeds, ginger, garlic, shiso and nori.

In a medium saucepan over a medium-high heat, bring the sesame oil up to a simmer. Toss in the ginger and garlic cloves, and cook for 2 minutes stirring occasionally. Add the soy sauce, fish sauce and lime leaf, and cook for a further minute.

Pour in the chicken stock, sesame seeds and mushrooms, and slowly bring back up to a simmer. Add the udon noodles and simmer for approximately 10 minutes.

While the noodles are cooking, poach the eggs and grill or fry the bacon. I poach eggs in a small frying pan, so you can see how cooked the yolk is. Fill the frying pan with enough water to just cover the eggs and add the white wine vinegar. Bring to the boil and then take off the heat; the eggs will continue to cook in the hot water. Once the eggs are cooked to your liking, and your bacon is done, the soup should be ready.

Ladle the udon noodle broth into bowls and sprinkle with coriander and spinach. Spoon a poached egg into each bowl, top with the bacon, drizzle with chilli and sesame oils, and sprinkle over a pinch of shichimi togarashi, if using.

THIN HERBY OMELETTE
with Feta & Coriander

SERVES 4

110 g (3¾ oz) fresh herbs, such as dill, parsley, chives, coriander (cilantro) and tarragon
5 eggs
1 teaspoon salt
freshly ground black pepper
100 ml (3½ fl oz) water
4 teaspoons olive oil
100 g (3½ oz) feta
handful of coriander leaves

If your herb garden or window box is growing at full throttle, this is a great omelette to create and use up some of those fresh herbs. Taught to me by a fantastic Belgian chef, these omelettes can be kept in the fridge for up to 24 hours, ready to warm up for whenever you need a quick feed.

Preheat the oven to 140°C (275°F/Gas 1). Chop your herbs, except for the coriander, as finely as you can; a mezzaluna is quite handy here to get a good chopping action going.

Crack all the eggs into a bowl, season with salt and pepper, and add the water. Give it a good whisk. Add the herbs and stir to combine.

Heat 1 teaspoon of the oil in a non-stick frying pan and imagine you are going to make a lovely thin crêpe. I find that by visualising this process it helps you get what you want. Add about 2 tablespoons of the mixture, or enough to coat the bottom of the pan evenly. A good size to aim for is 15 cm (6 in).

Cook undisturbed until the edges start to brown and the egg is just cooked through. You won't need to flip these as they are so thin. Carefully slide the omelette from the pan on to a baking sheet, crumble over some feta, add a few torn coriander leaves and roll up. Keep the omelettes warm in the oven until you are ready to serve.

I like to eat these with a simple fresh tomato salad.

GRIDDLED GRAPEFRUIT
with Pistachios & Yoghurt

SERVES 4

2 pink grapefruits

2 tablespoons orange–
blossom honey

2 pinches of cinnamon

1 tablespoon boiling water

handful of toasted
pistachio nuts

4 dessertspoons natural
yoghurt

If you are in a hurry or fancy something light, have a go at this warm citrus breakfast. It's very simple and very pleasing. Try adding other toasted nuts if you prefer.

Turn on the grill. Slice the grapefruits in half and pat the flesh dry with kitchen towel (kitchen paper). In a small bowl, dissolve the honey with the cinnamon and boiling water.

Line a baking tray with parchment paper. Arrange the grapefruit cut side up and drizzle with the honey mixture. Grill for 8–10 minutes until caramelised on top, but keep an eye on them to make sure they don't burn.

Serve with a dollop of yoghurt and sprinkle of pistachios.

NORWEGIAN APPLE SAUCE
with Rye Cinnamon Crumbs & Yoghurt

SERVES 4

FOR THE APPLE SAUCE

1.4 kg (3 lb 1 oz) cooking apples, peeled, cored and cut into 2 cm (1–in) chunks

juice of 1 lemon

1 stick cinnamon

60 g (2 oz/⅓ lightly packed cup) soft light brown sugar

100 ml (3½ fl oz) water

pinch of salt

FOR THE RYE CINNAMON CRUMBS

2 slices rye bread

40 g (1½ oz) butter

60 g (2 oz/⅓ lightly packed cup) soft dark brown sugar

½ teaspoon ground cinnamon, or more to taste

FOR THE VANILLA YOGHURT

1 vanilla pod, seeds scraped

200 ml (7 fl oz) plain yoghurt

This is a great alternative to a fruit compote and granola. It's a Nordic-style version, which means there's more cinnamon spice, a tiny bit of butter and brown sugar.

Start by making the apple sauce by combining all of the ingredients in a large, heavy-bottomed saucepan with a lid. On a high heat, bring it to a boil, then turn down the heat and simmer for approximately 20 minutes or until the apples are soft. Remove from the heat and discard the cinnamon stick. Mash the apples with a fork or potato masher until you have a good, soft consistency. Set to one side.

For the rye cinnamon crumbs, break the slices into small breadcrumbs with your fingers. You don't want the crumbs to be too fine, as you want them to have a nice bite. Transfer to a frying pan and stir in the rest of the ingredients. Fry over a medium heat, stirring continuously, for 5 minutes until the butter and sugar have caramelised and the bread has soaked up all the flavours. Tip them onto greaseproof paper and leave to cool. They will be crunchy on the outside once cooked.

To make the vanilla yoghurt, mix the vanilla seeds into the yoghurt and give it a stir.

Assemble by spooning some apple sauce into a bowl, then top with yoghurt and add a sprinkling of rye crumbs.

SMOKED SALMON & EGGS
with Capers & Quinoa Crackers

SERVES 2

FOR THE QUINOA CRACKERS (MAKES 24)

160 g (5½ oz) quinoa, soaked overnight in a covered bowl and drained

110 ml (4 fl oz) water

½ teaspoon sea salt

2 tablespoons olive oil

FOR THE TOPPING

1 tablespoon capers

handful of sorrel leaves

olive oil for frying

4 eggs

salt and freshly ground black pepper

1 apple (granny smith works best)

50–75 g (2–2½ oz) smoked salmon

All these bits make up a smoky, tangy, crunchy mouthful, which is rather delightful.

To make the crackers, preheat the oven to 180°C (350°F/Gas 4). Put the quinoa, water and salt into a food processor and whizz until you have a consistency like double (heavy) cream. If left to stand, the batter will thicken, so just add water to get it back to a creamy consistency.

Line a baking sheet with parchment paper, or you can use a muffin tin which you need to grease. If using a muffin tin, it needs to go into the oven for a few minutes to heat up before you add the mixture.

Using a tablespoon, put a dollop of the mixture on to the baking sheet or into the muffin tin. Continue spooning the batter on to the baking sheet, leaving 4 cm (1½ in) between each spoonful to allow the biscuits to spread as they cook. Bake for 15–20 minutes until golden and crisp on the bottom. Flip over each cracker and bake for a further 5–10 minutes.

To make the topping, start by frying the capers and sorrel in a little olive oil until crispy, then drain on a piece of kitchen towel (kitchen paper).

Whisk the eggs in a bowl and season. Add a little oil to a saucepan over a low heat and pour in the eggs. Stir slowly until the eggs are just scrambled. Remove from the heat.

Halve and core the apple, and slice each half into 5–6 segments.

I like to eat this by using the quinoa crackers as large spoons to scoop up spoonfuls of scrambled egg, then adding a little bit of salmon and a sprinkle of the crispy capers and sorrel over the top.

It is not vital that you are hungover to try the following recipes; I have merely given this chapter its name as I feel it sums up those comforting, nostalgic breakfasts that can make you feel content. I could have called it 'when you are feeling sorry for yourself', but, as you may agree, it doesn't have the same ring to it!

Your own favourite comforting breakfast can be very personal, and I only hope that these recipes touch you in some way. I am by no means trying to replace your favourite breakfast, but I hope to entice you to find something new.

MOROCCAN EGGS

SERVES 2

olive oil for frying

1 garlic clove, grated

1 red onion, finely chopped

1 teaspoon cumin seeds

½ teaspoon chilli powder

½ teaspoon chilli flakes
(spicy red pepper flakes)

1 × 400 g (14 oz) can chopped
tomatoes, or 3 fresh ripe
tomatoes, chopped

1 teaspoon salt

4 eggs

handful of coriander
(cilantro)

100 ml (3½ fl oz) natural
yoghurt to serve

I discovered this magical breakfast while working in a Riad – a traditional Moroccan house – in Fes. It's delicious with bread or toast. I often crave it, and I always have the ingredients in my cupboard just in case!

Pour a drizzle of oil into a frying pan and fry the garlic for 20 seconds over a medium heat so it flavours the oil, then add the onion. Fry for 3 minutes until the onion has softened, then stir in the cumin seeds, chilli powder and chilli flakes. After 1 more minute, add the tomatoes and salt. Stir and let this cook down for 3 minutes.

Using a wooden spoon, create 4 wells in the tomato sauce. Crack an egg into each well and then cover your frying pan with a lid. If you don't have a lid for the pan, you can use a baking tray to cover it instead. This helps the tops of the eggs to cook.

When the eggs are cooked to your liking, sprinkle with coriander and serve from the pan in the middle of the table. I love mine with a dollop of yoghurt to soothe the chilli just a little.

MEXICAN CORN HASH

2 tablespoons olive oil

1 red onion, finely chopped

1 garlic clove, grated

1 large courgette (zucchini), diced

2 cobs of corn, kernels removed from the core (see page 68) or 1 × 336 g (12 oz) can sweetcorn

1 large tomato, finely chopped

1 tablespoon chopped pickled jalapeños

salt and freshly ground black pepper

50 g (2 oz) feta, crumbled (optional)

2 eggs

squeeze of lime

This spicy little treat is quick to make and delicious when piled on to a tortilla with extra chilli sauce.

Heat 1 tablespoon of oil in a frying pan over a medium heat and add the onion. Fry for 2–3 minutes, then add the garlic, courgette and sweetcorn. Cook for a further 3–4 minutes until the corn and courgettes are slightly browned, then add the tomato and jalapeños and fry for another 3–4 minutes.

Remove from the heat and season with lots of pepper. If you are using feta, add this now so it melts slightly into the warm dish. Feta is quite salty, so it's best to add the salt after the feta, after giving it a taste first.

In a clean frying pan, heat 1 tablespoon of oil over a high heat and fry the eggs until cooked through.

Spoon your courgette and corn hash on to two plates and squeeze with lime. Place the fried egg on top and serve. I sometimes add some chipotle paste to mayonnaise to create a spicy condiment for this dish.

EGGS ON BUBBLE CAKES
with Black Pudding

SERVES 3-4

400 g (14 oz) mashed potato

2 tablespoons plain (all-purpose) flour, plus extra for dusting

1 teaspoon baking powder

120 g (4 oz) cooked greens, such as cabbage or brussels sprouts, chopped

2 tablespoons chopped chives

50 g (2 oz) black pudding

5–6 eggs

salt and freshly ground black pepper

1 tablespoon olive oil

1 teaspoon butter

1 tablespoon white wine vinegar

Next time you are thinking about throwing some leftover mash away or giving it to the dog, don't. These little crispy potato cakes should spring to mind. Full of flavour from the black pudding, they're delicious eaten with egg oozing out over the top.

Preheat the oven to 140°C (275°F/Gas 1). Put the mashed potato into a large bowl, sieve in the flour and baking powder and mix together. Add the greens and chives, crumble in the black pudding and season. Stir to combine. Add 2 of the eggs and mix all the ingredients together until smooth and firm.

Shape the cakes using your hands and dust each one with flour. Heat a large frying pan over a medium heat, add the oil and butter and fry the patties in batches for around 3 minutes on each side or until they are golden brown. Keep warm in the oven. Repeat until you have cooked all the cakes.

To poach the eggs, fill a frying pan with water up to 2 cm (¾ in) and bring the water to a simmer. Add a tablespoon of white wine vinegar and crack your eggs into the pan. Bring the water up to the boil and cook your eggs for 1 minute then turn the heat down and simmer for a further 3 minutes. Splash the top of the eggs with the water if they need a bit more cooking using a spatula place them on top of your cakes and serve.

PROSCIUTTO, CHILLI, EGGS & ROCKET

2 tablespoons olive oil, plus extra for drizzling

1 small red onion, roughly chopped

2 slices prosciutto, cut into 1 cm (½ in) cubes

2 slices bread, cut into 1 cm (½ in) cubes

1 red chilli, chopped

1 tomato, halved, seeds removed and chopped

1 teaspoon salt, plus more for seasoning

1 tablespoon sherry vinegar, or ½ teaspoon lemon juice

4 eggs

2 handfuls of rocket (arugula)

1 tablespoon chopped parsley

freshly ground black pepper

I have developed this recipe over the years, adapting it to reflect where we have lived and worked. We spend a lot of time in Italy, and with all the fantastic ingredients there, the name 'Italian Eggs' is currently sticking.

Pour 1 tablespoon of the oil into a frying pan over a medium heat. Tip in the onion and fry for around 2–3 minutes until translucent. Add the prosciutto, bread and chilli. Drizzle over another tablespoon of oil to help the bread crisp up; we want a nice crunchy texture to the finished croutons for this recipe. Fry for about 3 minutes, stirring occasionally until the bread is just crispy. Add the tomato, salt and vinegar, give it a good stir and cook for a further 30 seconds.

Make 4 little wells in the mixture in the frying pan. Crack an egg into a small cup and tip it into one of the wells; I find doing this, rather than cracking the eggs directly into the wells, reduces the possibility of breaking the egg yolk. Do this for the rest of the eggs. The egg white will slightly disperse in the pan, bringing the croutons together. Put the lid on the frying pan to speed up the eggs' cooking time; if you don't have a lid then use a baking tray to cover the pan. Cook for 2–3 minutes or until the eggs are cooked to your liking.

Tip the ingredients on to a plate; they should slide off the frying pan happily. Top with rocket and parsley, then season with salt and pepper and a drizzle of olive oil.

BANANA PANCAKES

2 eggs

2 small ripe bananas, peeled

85 g (3 oz) butter, melted, plus extra for frying

240 ml (8½ fl oz) milk

½ teaspoon vanilla extract

2 tablespoons sugar

¼ teaspoon salt

3 teaspoons baking powder

200 g (7 oz/scant 1⅔ cups) plain (all-purpose) flour

olive oil for frying

These are extremely quick to make and taste sensational, especially when using over-ripe bananas. I sometimes serve them up with some maple bacon to get that salty-sweet flavour that I love.

Preheat the oven to 140°C (275°F/Gas 1). Crack your eggs into a mixing bowl and mash in the banana using the back of a fork. Stir in the melted butter, milk and vanilla extract. Add the rest of the ingredients and whisk well to combine; you should have a smooth batter consistency with bits of banana. If you want to make this in advance, make up the batter without the baking powder and store it in the fridge. Add the baking powder just before you want to cook the pancakes.

Melt a knob of butter with a small drizzle of olive oil in a frying pan over a medium-high heat. Like with all pancakes, the first one never comes out how you want it to, but see how you get on. You want to make these pancakes small and thick, rather than big and thin, so spoon about 2 tablespoons of batter into the hot pan. Fry for 2–3 minutes until bubbles form on top. Flip over and cook on the other side for up to a minute until it is golden brown. Slide on to a plate and keep warm in the oven.

Depending on the size of your pan, make your pancakes in batches. These are delicious eaten as soon as possible.

SAUSAGE FLATBREAD
with Egg & Harissa Yoghurt

SERVES 2

2 sausages (I use spicy or herby ones)

1 tablespoon olive oil

2 tablespoons tomato purée (tomato paste)

1 large or two small flatbread(s)

6 cherry tomatoes, chopped

2 eggs

2 tablespoons grated mozzarella

2 teaspoons harissa paste

4 tablespoons natural yoghurt

handful of chopped parsley

This can sometimes be referred to as a pizza because of the way it looks, but I just can't bring myself to call it that! Either way, it tastes damn good.

Preheat the oven to 180°C (350°F/Gas 4) and line a baking tray big enough to fit the flatbread in with baking parchment.

Remove the skins from the sausages and add the oil to a frying pan over a medium heat. Fry the sausages, breaking up the sausage meat with a wooden spoon, for about 5 minutes until just crisping up. Take off the heat and leave to one side.

Spread the tomato purée evenly over the flatbread using a knife or the back of spoon. Sprinkle the chopped cherry tomatoes over the top and put the flatbread in the oven for 3 minutes to warm it up slightly.

Remove from the oven and add the fried sausage pieces to the top of the flatbread. Crack the eggs on top and sprinkle with mozzarella. Put the flatbread back in the oven and cook for 8 minutes until the eggs are cooked through.

Meanwhile make the harissa yoghurt by mixing the harissa paste with the yoghurt in a bowl. Remove the flatbread from the oven, sprinkle with parsley and serve with the harissa yoghurt.

MY FRY-UP

100 g (3½ oz) smoked streaky bacon or smoked pancetta, cut into 1 cm (½ in) cubes

6 cherry tomatoes, halved and seeds removed

2 field mushrooms, sliced

1 × 320 g (11½ oz) roll ready-made butter puff pastry

4 sun-dried tomatoes, chopped

4 eggs, boiled for 6 minutes in boiling water and halved

olive oil

2 slices white bread

handful of chopped parsley

salt and freshly ground black pepper

I was toying with the idea of putting my version of an English fry-up in this book, but I felt that because everyone has their own favourite fry-up ingredients, I wouldn't be able to tempt you to try another way! Instead I've included this recipe, where you can change the toppings to suit your tastes but serve them in a slightly different way.

Turn the grill on to high. Spread the bacon, tomatoes and mushrooms evenly on to a baking tray and grill for 3–4 minutes, turning once, then take them out and set aside.

Preheat the oven to 200°C (400°F/Gas 6) and line another baking tray with baking parchment. Roll out the pastry to around 350 mm × 225 mm (14 in × 9 in), and lay it on the parchment. Using a fork, prick the pastry all over to prevent it from rising when it cooks. Bake in the oven for 5 minutes then remove.

Arrange the sun-dried tomatoes evenly over the pastry. Then add the bacon, tomatoes and mushrooms and top with the boiled eggs. Brush all over with a little oil and bake for a further 8–10 minutes, until the pastry is golden brown.

While the tart is cooking, whizz the white bread in a food processor, add the chopped parsley and season. Crisp the mixture up in a frying pan with a teaspoon of oil.

Serve with the parsley crumbs sprinkled over the top and your choice of sauces.

STREAKY BACON
with Creamed Corn on Hash Browns

SERVES 2

FOR THE CREAMED CORN

3 fresh cobs of corn

120 ml (4 fl oz) water

40 g (1½ oz) unsalted butter

2 teaspoons sugar

salt and freshly ground black pepper

50 ml (2 fl oz) crème fraîche

1 teaspoon Tabasco (hot-pepper sauce) (optional)

FOR THE HASH BROWNS

1 large potato

¼ teaspoon salt

freshly ground black pepper

1 tablespoon butter

8 cherry tomatoes on the vine

4 rashers (slices) smoked streaky bacon

Hash browns are liked by everyone and are irresistible when made from scratch. Don't go buying the frozen variety that look like mini sponges. You can make the hash browns in advance, just put them in the frying pan to crisp them back up again.

Make the creamed corn by cutting the kernels from the core of the cob. Do this by peeling off and removing the husk and the silky threads that cover the corn, then stand the cob stalk-end down on a chopping board and carefully slice the kernels off from top to bottom using a sharp knife. Cut as close to the core as possible so that the kernels remain whole. Careful here of your fingers, as well as the mess. Some kernels take flight and decide to miss your chopping board, and end up somewhere you might find them a few days later! Once you have removed all the corn, put the kernels into a saucepan with the water, butter and sugar. Season generously with salt and pepper.

Bring up to a gentle simmer on a medium heat, and cook for about 20–25 minutes until the corn is soft. Strain the cooking liquid into a bowl or jug. Transfer half the cooked corn into another bowl, and tip the rest into a food processor and blend until smooth. If you want it to be super-smooth, pass it through a really fine sieve after blending. If you find it is a bit thick, you can add a little of the reserved cooking liquid to loosen it. Stir the puréed corn into the rest of the corn, and add the crème fraîche and Tabasco (if using). Check the seasoning and keep warm.

Now for those hash browns. Peel and grate the potato into a bowl lined with a clean tea towel (kitchen towel). Perhaps choose a tea towel you don't particularly like, so you don't mind squeezing hard – it's therapeutic! Gather the tea towel around the potato and twist the neck to form a tight package. Continue twisting the cloth and squishing the liquid out of the potato as much as you can. The more you squeeze, the better the hash brown!

In a heavy-bottomed frying pan or a skillet, melt the butter over a medium-high heat, then add a large spoonful of the potatoes. Depending on how big your pan is, use half the mixture for each hash brown and flatten each portion using the back of a spatula. Fry for 3–4 minutes until it looks crisp and golden, then flip over and fry for a further 2–3 minutes until you have a lovely golden-brown hash.

Preheat the oven to 180°C (350°F/Gas 4). Pop the tomatoes on a baking tray and roast in the oven for 5 minutes. Meanwhile, fry the bacon until crispy. Put the hash browns in the oven for a few minutes just to warm up. Serve up the hash browns, topped with the creamed corn, bacon and tomatoes. I've been known to sprinkle this with fresh chopped chilli and serve with a salsa made of chopped avocado, red onion and tomato on the side, but eat as it suits you.

SCRAMBLED HASH
with Black-eyed Beans

SERVES 2

FOR THE HASH

½ × 400 g (14 oz) can cooked black-eyed beans (black-eyed peas), drained

olive oil for frying

1 large potato, peeled and cut into 1 cm (½ in) cubes

3 eggs

1 tablespoon milk

½ teaspoon salt

½ teaspoon chilli flakes (spicy red pepper flakes)

2 handfuls of chopped coriander (cilantro)

2 spring onions (scallions), thinly sliced

2 tablespoons grated Cheddar

FOR THE TOMATO SALSA

200 g (7 oz) cherry tomatoes, chopped

½ red onion, finely chopped

1 chilli, halved, seeds removed and finely chopped

handful of mint leaves, roughly chopped

½ teaspoon sugar

1 tablespoon red wine vinegar

2 tablespoons extra-virgin olive oil

salt and freshly ground black pepper

toast to serve

In some areas of southern USA, it's a tradition to eat black-eyed beans (called black-eyed peas in the US) in the New Year to bring in good fortune for the coming year. This dish deserves to be eaten more than once a year, but don't worry if you do – it won't cancel out your good fortune, I promise!

Using the back of a fork, mash the black-eyed beans a little in a bowl. This gives an added texture to the dish.

Cook the potato in a frying pan with 1 tablespoon of olive oil and enough water to cover it. Bring to the boil, then turn down the heat and simmer until all the water has evaporated. The potato should be tender and slightly browned with just the oil left in the pan. Stir in the black-eyed beans and let the potato and beans crisp up a little. If you find the mixture is drying out, just add a little bit more oil.

Meanwhile, put the eggs, milk, salt, chilli flakes and 1 handful of chopped coriander into a bowl and whisk together. Tip the egg mixture into the pan over the potatoes and beans, add the spring onions and mix together.

Continue to slowly stir the scramble and cook for about 3 minutes until the eggs are set and then sprinkle with the cheese. Remove from the heat and quickly make the tomato salsa by combining all the ingredients together in a bowl. Top the scramble with the rest of the coriander and serve with toast and the tomato salsa.

TURKEY PATTIES
with Maple Bacon

SERVES 4

2 slices stale white bread

450 g (1 lb) minced (ground) turkey

1 garlic clove, grated

1 egg

4 spring onions (scallions), finely sliced

2 tablespoons finely chopped parsley

1½ teaspoons salt

½ teaspoon freshly ground black pepper

oil for frying

8 rashers (slices) streaky bacon

2 tablespoons maple syrup

eggs, cooked any style, to serve

These pair up well with any type of eggs you fancy, from scrambled to boiled. Maple bacon can turn into addiction. You have been warned.

Preheat the oven to 200°C (400°F/Gas 6). For the patties, soak the bread in a bowl of cold water for 1 minute, then squeeze out the water and crumble the bread into a large bowl. Add the turkey, garlic, egg, spring onions, parsley and seasoning, and combine everything together. With wet hands, shape the mixture into 8 golf balls and flatten into patties using the palm of your hand.

Add enough oil to shallow fry the patties in to a large frying pan. Heat the oil and then fry the patties – in batches if necessary – for about 4–5 minutes on each side until they are cooked through and golden brown all over.

While the patties are frying, prepare the bacon. Line a baking tray with baking parchment and lay on the bacon. Bake for about 15 minutes until crispy and just beginning to brown.

Keep an eye on the patties as the bacon cooks, and when the patties are done remove them from the pan and set aside to drain on some kitchen towel (kitchen paper).

Take the bacon out of the oven and, using a pastry brush, coat the bacon with the maple syrup. Put the bacon back in the oven for 3–5 minutes until it has browned and is sticky. Meanwhile, cook some eggs in your preferred style; you may have to remove the bacon from the oven and set it to one side with the patties for a few minutes while you finish cooking your eggs.

Serve the turkey patties and maple bacon with the eggs.

The recipes in this section are those that you
give in to. Ones you can't help but make again and again when
you want a treat or to be generous. Feed the people you
care about with this selection of dishes and, between you and
me, watch your popularity increase dramatically.

INDULGENT

Smoked Trout, Ricotta & New Potato
ROLLED OMELETTE

SERVES 4

150 g (5 oz) new potatoes,
quartered

olive oil

150 g (5 oz) ricotta

½ teaspoon horseradish
cream

60 g (2 oz) Parmesan, grated

salt and freshly ground
black pepper

8 eggs

100 g (3½ oz) watercress

200 g (7 oz) smoked trout,
flaked

This flexible dish can also be served up as a light lunch along with a well-dressed crispy green salad. Using ricotta as your base cheese, you can experiment with lots of fillings, depending on what you have in the fridge. Another combination I use regularly is butternut squash, sage and prosciutto.

Boil the new potatoes in a large saucepan for 5 minutes and then drain. Heat a large frying pan and add 2 tablespoons of olive oil. Fry the potatoes for about 10 minutes, turning them occasionally, until golden and crispy, and set to one side.

Meanwhile, combine the ricotta, horseradish, half of the Parmesan and a good grinding of salt and pepper in a bowl. Break the eggs into another bowl, season and beat lightly. Heat a little olive oil in a large frying pan over a medium heat, and pour in half of the beaten egg. Cook for 6–8 minutes until the egg has just set. Slide the omelette out of the pan and on to a baking tray lined with baking parchment. Make a second omelette with the rest of the egg and slide this next to the first one so they slightly overlap and create 'figure of eight' omelette.

Spoon the ricotta mixture in a line along the middle of both omelettes. Top with the potatoes, flaked fish and then the watercress.

Turn on the grill to heat up and carefully roll up the omelette to make one big rolled omelette. Start from one of the longer ends and fold the omelette over the filling, then gently roll it over, tucking in the omelette as you go. Sprinkle with the rest of the Parmesan and put under the grill for 3 minutes. Slice it up into 7.5 cm (3 in) pieces and serve.

BLUEBERRY ALMOND PANCAKES
with Cinnamon Sauce

MAKES ABOUT 20 PANCAKES

FOR THE CINNAMON SAUCE

175 g (6 oz/scant 1 lightly packed cup) soft brown sugar

1 tablespoon cornflour (corn starch)

240 ml (8½ fl oz) boiling water

2 tablespoons salted butter

1 teaspoon vanilla extract

¾ teaspoon ground cinnamon

FOR THE PANCAKES

3 eggs

60 ml (2 fl oz) buttermilk, plus extra if necessary

1 tablespoon melted unsalted butter

1 tablespoon maple syrup

1 teaspoon vanilla extract

225 g (8 oz) ground almonds

pinch of salt

½ teaspoon bicarbonate of soda

100 g (3½ oz) blueberries

butter for frying

These delicious gluten-free fluffy pancakes are made with ground almonds and are bursting with warm berries. Cinnamon is not to everyone's taste, so you could replace it with a vanilla pod, which you add to the sauce at the same time as the butter (before simmering) instead. This is also delicious as a dessert served with ice cream.

To make the sauce, put the sugar and cornflour in a saucepan over a medium heat and slowly add the water, stirring until thickened. Add the butter and simmer for 6–8 minutes. Remove from the heat and whisk in the vanilla and cinnamon. Set aside while you make the pancakes.

For the pancakes, heat a heavy-based frying pan to a medium heat. Meanwhile, put all the ingredients except the blueberries and butter into a food processor and blend. The batter should come out relatively thick, like whipped double cream.

Pour the batter into a mixing bowl and fold in the blueberries. If you find that it doesn't pour as it is very thick, just add a little bit more buttermilk to loosen the mixture.

Add a small knob of butter to the hot frying pan and, using a serving spoon, put a dollop of the batter into the pan. Cook for 3–4 minutes until the edges dry out and the underneath turns a golden brown. Flip and cook for a further 2 minutes until cooked through. Fry the pancakes in batches, keeping the cooked ones warm in a low oven, or serve as and when they are done, drizzled with cinnamon sauce.

FRIED CHOCOLATE BREAD

SERVES 4

100 g (3½ oz) unsalted butter, softened

16 slices French baguette, cut on the diagonal

100 g (3½ oz) milk chocolate, broken into pieces

These delicious chocolate sandwiches can be made in minutes. Buttery and crunchy with chocolate oozing out of the edges, this provides you with a sweet, indulgent breakfast. I recommend dipping them in your hot breakfast drink of choice. I like mine dipped in a spicy chai.

Butter one side of the baguette slices generously. Place 8 slices, buttered side down, on a piece of baking parchment on a work surface and cover each slice with chocolate, leaving a little space around the edges to allow for the chocolate melting. Top each slice with another slice of baguette, this time, buttered side up.

Heat up a heavy-based frying pan or a skillet and fry the sandwiches in batches. Fry for about 3–4 minutes on each side, turning over once, until they are golden. Pile the golden chocolate sarnies high on a plate and serve – causing a frenzy.

BEEF, CHARD & EGG CASSEROLE

SERVES 4

FOR THE TAHINI DRESSING

150 ml (5 fl oz) tahini

70 ml (2½ fl oz) lemon juice

150 ml (5 fl oz) water

1 garlic clove, grated

salt to taste

30 g (1 oz) flat-leaf parsley, chopped

FOR THE CASSEROLE

olive oil for frying

1 red onion, finely chopped

400 g (14 oz) lean minced (ground) beef

2 garlic cloves, grated

1 teaspoon chilli flakes (spicy red pepper flakes)

1 tablespoon tomato purée (tomato paste)

2 tablespoons water

200 g (7 oz) Swiss chard, roughly chopped

4 duck eggs

This is a delicious, Lebanese-inspired dish served with a tahini yoghurt-style dressing. It's the dressing that takes it up a notch, and brings you back into the kitchen to make it again and again. The dressing can happily keep in your fridge for three days – but don't add the parsley until just before you are ready to use it – and is also great with oily fish and roasted vegetables. I love using Swiss chard for this dish, which is in season between July and November, but you can use any kind of chard you like.

Make the dressing by whisking together the tahini, lemon juice, water and garlic in a bowl until you have a creamy, smooth texture. Add salt to taste and set aside.

To make the casserole, preheat the oven to 180°C (350°F/Gas 4). Pour 1 tablespoon of oil into a large frying pan over a medium heat and then add the onion. Fry the onion for 3–4 minutes until it is translucent. Add the mince and half of the garlic to the pan, and fry for 5 minutes before adding the chilli flakes and tomato purée. Continue to cook for around another 10 minutes, stirring occasionally, until the beef is a little crispy and brown in colour. Sometimes a bit of water leaches out from the mince, so if this happens just turn up the heat and allow the water to evaporate, then reduce the heat back to medium and carry on browning the beef. Spoon the mince mixture into a shallow casserole dish and set aside.

Pour another tablespoon of oil into the frying pan and add the rest of the garlic. When the garlic starts to sizzle, add the chard; it may look quite a lot at first, but don't worry, it does cook down. Fry the chard for 5–8 minutes, stirring now and again, until it has wilted down, then spoon it into the casserole dish.

Combine the chard with the mince and spread the mixture evenly across the bottom of the dish, then make 4 large wells. Crack the eggs carefully into the wells, cover the dish with foil and then bake in the oven for 10 minutes. Remove the foil and serve at the table with the tahini dressing; stir the parsley through the dressing just before you serve.

CURRIED SCRAMBLED EGGS
with Smoked Haddock & Tomato Chilli Jam

SERVES 4

200 g (7 oz) undyed smoked haddock

1 tablespoon olive oil

1 red onion, finely diced

1 green chilli, seeds removed and finely diced

½ teaspoon hot red chilli powder

2 medium tomatoes, seeds removed and finely chopped

5 eggs, whisked

small bunch of coriander (cilantro), roughly chopped

FOR THE TOMATO CHILLI JAM

1 teaspoon olive oil

1 medium onion, finely chopped

2 medium tomatoes, roughly chopped

8 cherry tomatoes, halved

1 red chilli, seeds removed and finely diced

100 g (3½ oz/generous ½ lightly packed cup) light brown sugar

1 teaspoon grated ginger

2 star anise

1 teaspoon soy sauce

1 teaspoon white wine vinegar

A twist on the classic breakfast dish, kedgeree. I love eggs and spices, and this dish goes so well with smoked fish, in this case haddock. I like to get a lot of charred lines on my bread to go with it, as I want it to take me back to a café in Mumbai.

To make the tomato chilli jam, put the oil and onion into a large high-sided frying pan over a medium heat and fry for 1 minute. Add all of the tomatoes and the chilli, and cook for about 2–3 minutes. Add the rest of the ingredients and cook for a further 30–40 minutes, stirring periodically to make sure the jam doesn't stick to the bottom of the pan. After you've added the sugar, you will notice that the jam becomes sticky and shiny. Remove from the heat and leave to cool. Pour into a food processor and whizz up to make a smooth consistency. You can store the jam in a sterilised jam jar in the fridge up to 2 weeks, but it only lasts about 2 days in our house.

For the scramble, put the haddock into a saucepan, cover generously with water and bring to a simmer over a medium heat. Simmer for 4 minutes or until the fish is opaque and cooked through. Using a slotted spoon, lift the fish out from the pan and flake it into large pieces into a bowl. Set to one side.

Heat the oil in a non-stick frying pan over a medium heat and add the onion. Fry for around 2–3 minutes until translucent. Add the chilli and chilli powder, followed by the tomatoes. Cook for a further 2 minutes and then stir in the eggs and coriander. Increase the heat to cook the eggs through, which should take about 2–3 minutes. Remove from the heat and gently stir the fish into the eggs.

Serve with griddled bread and the tomato chilli jam.

TURKISH EGGS,
Yoghurt & Chilli Butter

SERVES 6

2 tablespoons white wine vinegar

6 medium eggs

600 ml (1 pint) Greek or home-made yoghurt (see page 30)

200 ml (7 fl oz) double (heavy) cream

zest and juice of 1 lemon

salt and freshly ground black pepper

75 g (2½ oz) salted butter

½ teaspoon chilli powder

¼ teaspoon hot smoked paprika

1 red chilli, finely chopped

small bunch of parsley, chopped

mini pittas, toasted and sliced, to serve

Eggs are very much a staple in Turkish cooking, along with yoghurt. This dish is surprisingly indulgent, using comforting ingredients and adding a little spice. It is the oozing nature of every mouthful that sends you off on a journey of wonderment.

Poach the eggs by filling a large high-sided frying pan with about 4 cm (1½ in) of water over a medium heat and add the vinegar. Crack the eggs into the water, making sure they are evenly spaced. Bring the water to the boil, then take off the heat. The eggs should stay warm while you are preparing everything else. If you find the tops of the eggs need cooking a bit more, just splash some of the hot water over them or put a lid or baking tray over the pan when you cook them to slightly steam the tops.

Pour the yoghurt and cream into a mixing bowl, stir in the lemon juice and zest, and season. Whisk until stiff and then divide equally between 6 bowls.

In a separate frying pan, melt the butter with the chilli powder and paprika, and let it bubble for 3–4 minutes. Remove from the heat before the butter turns brown.

Use a slotted spoon to put an egg on top of the yoghurt in each bowl, then spoon over the butter and sprinkle with chilli and parsley. Serve with the toasted pitta breads.

CHUNKY CINNAMON TOASTS
with Blackberry Compôte

SERVES 2–3

FOR THE BERRY COMPÔTE

250 g (9 oz) blackberries

2–3 tablespoons granulated sugar

squeeze of lemon

FOR THE CINNAMON TOAST

50 g (2 oz/generous ¼ lightly packed cup) soft light brown sugar

1 teaspoon ground cinnamon

6 thick slices white bread

softened salted butter

crème fraîche to serve

You need a lovely fluffy white bloomer for this recipe and feel free to use frozen blackberries if they are not in season, just add a bit more sugar to taste.

Make the berry compôte by placing the berries, sugar and lemon juice in a saucepan, and slowly bring to a simmer. Simmer for 3–4 minutes and then take off the heat.

For the cinnamon toast, mix the sugar and cinnamon together in a bowl. Toast the bread under the grill, then butter it generously on one side while it is still warm. Sprinkle over over the cinnamon sugar and return the toast to the grill until the sugar starts to bubble. Remove from the grill and plate up with a spoonful of compôte and a dollop of crème fraîche. Delicious.

HOME-MADE MUFFINS
with Eggs Benedict

SERVES 4

FOR THE ENGLISH MUFFINS (MAKES 8 MUFFINS)

1¼ teaspoons active dry yeast

60 ml (2 fl oz) warm water

½ tablespoon caster (superfine) sugar

180 ml (6½ fl oz) whole milk

335 g (11¾ oz) strong white bread flour, plus extra for dusting

¾ teaspoon salt

1 tablespoon unsalted softened butter

oil for greasing

4 eggs

1 tablespoon white wine vinegar

4 thick slices cooked ham hock

hollandaise sauce (see page 90)

cayenne pepper to serve

This is definitely the most requested breakfast wherever I have worked. Ask various folk what their favorite breakfast is and this is always their go-to mid-morning weekend staple. I don't know why I am surprised, it is delicious, and here we have my classic version. For Florentine swap the ham for wilted spinach, for Royale swap in slices of smoked salmon. The muffins can be made in advance, kept in the fridge for up to a week or even freeze them.

For the muffins, stir the yeast into the warm water with a pinch of sugar in a bowl. Allow the yeast to dissolve a little and then add the milk. In another bowl, combine the flour, the remaining sugar and the salt, then mix in the butter. Pour in the yeast mixture and stir until the mixture clumps together and forms a ball of dough.

Sprinkle some flour over a clean work surface and scrape the dough out on to it. Knead the dough for about 8–10 minutes until it becomes elastic. Transfer to a lightly oiled bowl, cover with a clean tea towel and leave in a warm place for 1–1½ hours until the dough has doubled in size.

Flour a clean work surface and tip the dough out on to it. Divide the dough into 8 equal-sized pieces and then roll each one into a ball. Line a baking sheet with baking parchment and place the balls on to it. Cover with the tea towel again and allow to rise for another hour somewhere warm.

Preheat the oven to 200°C (400°F/Gas 6). Gently pat the dough balls down to make into muffin shapes. Put a heavy-based frying pan over medium heat and cook the muffins in the pan for 5–6 minutes on each side. You want them to be brown but not burnt.

Transfer the muffins to a baking tray and cook in the oven for a further 10–12 minutes.

While the muffins are baking, poach the eggs. Add 2 cm (¾ in) water to a frying pan. Stir in a dash of whit wine vinegar and bring the water to a simmer. Crack the eggs into the water, bring to the and cook for 1 minute boil. Once boiling, take the pan off the heat and let the eggs sit in the water until cooked to your liking.

Remove the muffins from the oven, split 4 of them in half and put the bottom halves on to plates. Top each half with a slice of ham, a poached egg and lashings of hollandaise. Sprinkle with cayenne pepper.

SMOKED SALMON CROQUETTES
with Hollandaise

MAKES 18 CROQUETTES

FOR THE CROQUETTES

500 ml (17 fl oz) whole milk

2 bay leaves

10 black peppercorns

½ onion, peeled

85 g (3 oz) butter

1 tablespoon olive oil

120 g (4 oz) smoked salmon, finely chopped

70 g (2½ oz/generous ½ cup) plain (all-purpose) flour, plus 4 tablespoons for frying

pinch of sea salt

1 litre sunflower oil for frying

2 eggs, beaten

250 g (9 oz) panko breadcrumbs

FOR THE HOLLANDAISE SAUCE

2 egg yolks

1 teaspoon white wine vinegar

pinch of salt

pinch of cayenne pepper

110 g (3¾ oz) cold butter, cubed

These creamy, smoky parcels of crunch and pillowy softness are great for a Christmas Day morning snack, or as canapés to start your evening off. Breakfast like a king, they say ...

For the croquettes, put the milk, bay leaves, peppercorns and onion into a saucepan and slowly bring it to the boil. Set aside for 1 hour to allow the flavours to infuse and the milk to cool. Strain the milk into a jug.

Melt the butter with the olive oil in a saucepan and then add the salmon. Cook for 3 minutes, then reduce the heat to low and stir in 70 g (2½ oz) of the flour and the salt. Beat for 5 minutes or until smooth. Slowly add the infused milk, 2–3 tablespoons at a time. Stir between each addition, continuing until the milk is fully incorporated. Cook for a further 5 minutes, stirring constantly, until the sauce is thick and smooth.

Pour the sauce into a cold baking tray or dish, and set aside for about 30–45 minutes to cool and set.

Use a dessertspoon to scoop up some set sauce and use a second dessertspoon to shape the sauce into a quenelle – an egg shape with tapered ends. Put the quenelle on to a lined tray and repeat with the rest of the sauce. Refrigerate for at least an hour.

For the hollandaise, fill a saucepan with just enough boiling water so that when you place a heatproof bowl on the pan, the water doesn't touch the bottom of the bowl. Place the saucepan over a high heat to keep the water simmering. Add the egg yolks, vinegar, salt and cayenne pepper to the bowl and whisk to combine. Slowly whisk in the butter, a cube at a time, until you have a lovely thick pale sauce. You can keep the sauce warm in the bowl over a low simmer until you're ready to serve up your croquettes.

To fry the croquettes, heat the oil in a large saucepan over a medium heat until a piece of bread dropped into the oil goes golden brown in 30 seconds. Meanwhile, pour the whisked eggs into a shallow bowl. Put the 4 tablespoons of flour on to a plate and the panko breadcrumbs on to a separate plate. Roll each croquette in the flour, then the egg, then the breadcrumbs, and set aside on some baking parchment. Once you have breadcrumbed all the croquettes, carefully add them to the hot oil. Fry for about 4 minutes or until golden brown, then remove and drain on some pieces of kitchen towel (kitchen paper). Serve with the hollandaise.

BOMBOLONI ALLA NUTELLA

MAKES
25 DOUGHNUTS

150 ml (5 fl oz) whole milk

15 g (½ oz) fast-action yeast

420 g (3⅓ cups) plain (all-purpose) flour, plus extra for dusting

80 g (3 oz) caster (superfine) sugar

2 eggs

zest of 1 lemon

pinch of salt

65 g (2¼ oz) unsalted butter, at room temperature

400 g (14 oz) Nutella

1.5 litres (3 pints 3 fl oz) vegetable oil for frying

icing sugar to serve

These very tempting Italian doughnuts are filled with Nutella, though they are just as good with jam or vanilla crème. Try including nuts for some added crunch.

Pour the milk into a small mixing bowl, add the yeast and gently stir, then set aside.

Put the flour, caster sugar, 1 whole egg and 1 egg yolk (keep the white for later), lemon zest and a pinch of salt into a large mixing bowl. Pour in the milk mixture and mix it in to form a dough.

Use a dough hook or knead by hand for 8–10 minutes until the dough is soft and supple. Add the butter and knead for another 8–10 minutes. Cover the bowl with a damp tea towel (kitchen towel) and leave for 2 hours to rise until it doubles in size.

Knead the dough again for 8–10 minutes and then roll it out to 5 mm (¼ in) thick on a floured work surface. You might find the dough quite elastic and therefore difficult to roll out, but persist with your rolling pin. Use a 5 cm (2 in) biscuit cutter to cut your dough into 50 circles. Spoon 1 teaspoon of Nutella on to a circle (use another spoon to scrape the Nutella off the teaspoon) and brush the edges with some of the beaten egg white you reserved earlier. Place another circle on top and gently push down around the edges to seal. Repeat this for the remaining circles to make 25 doughnuts. Leave to rest for around 10 minutes.

Meanwhile, heat the oil in a large saucepan to approximately 180°C (360°F). Use a slotted spoon to carefully place 3 bomboloni in the oil – cook no more than 3 at a time. Fry for 1 minute; they will puff up and turn a golden colour. Turn the bomboloni over with a spoon and fry the other side for another minute or until browned. Remove with the slotted spoon and drain on some kitchen towel (kitchen paper). Continue frying the remaining bomboloni.

Use a sieve to dust the finished bomboloni with icing sugar. Buon Appetito.

The smell of anything baking in the oven wafts up the staircase, buries itself under your nose and wakes up your stomach with a smile. I like to think that these are the recipes that do that.

BAKED

CHUNKY CARDAMOM & CINNAMON SWIRLY BUNS

MAKES 12 BUNS

FOR THE DOUGH

500 g (1 lb 2 oz/4 cups) strong white flour, plus extra for dusting

1 teaspoon salt

50 g (2 oz/generous ¼ lightly packed cup) light brown sugar

½ teaspoon dried yeast

75 g (2½ oz) unsalted butter, softened

200 ml (7 fl oz) whole milk

2 eggs, plus 1 yolk

oil for greasing

FOR THE FILLING

32 cardamom pods

100 g (3½ oz) hazelnuts

50 g (2 oz) demerara sugar, plus 2 tablespoons to serve

100 g (3½ oz) unsalted butter, softened

pinch of salt

1 teaspoon ground cinnamon

1–2 teaspoons poppy seeds

The soft, rich, buttery dough, along with the special nutty spice mix, give these buns the deliciousness you need some mornings, or afternoons for that matter.

To make the dough, combine the flour, salt and sugar in a bowl and stir in the yeast. Using your fingertips, rub the butter into the flour mixture until no clumps of butter are left.

Make a well in the mixture, pour in the milk and crack 1 egg into it. Mix the flour into the milk and egg, and bring the dough together to create a soft, supple texture – I find a spatula is good to mix the dough together with, instead of using warm hands. Turn the dough out on to a clean work surface dusted with a little flour. Knead for 10 minutes until smooth and elastic. Cut off a small piece and stretch it out to create a 'window'; you should be able to see the shadow of your fingers through it when it is ready. Place the dough into a lightly-oiled bowl, cover with a damp tea towel (kitchen towel) and leave for 1–1½ hours until doubled in size.

For the filling, split the cardamom pods and finely grind the seeds using a pestle and mortar. Whizz with the hazelnuts in a food processor until finely chopped. Mix 50 g (2 oz) of the sugar with the butter, cardamom, hazelnuts and salt in a bowl.

In another bowl mix the cinnamon with the 2 tablespoons of sugar, and scatter the mixture on to a baking sheet lined with baking parchment, ready for the dough.

Grease the base of a deep 34 × 24 cm (13 × 9 in) roasting tin and line with baking parchment. Knock the dough back and roll it out on a lightly floured work surface into a rectangle about 5 mm (¼ in) thick. Carefully pick up the dough and lay it over the cinnamon sugar mix. Spread the hazelnut mixture over the top of the dough, all the way to the edges.

Starting with the long edge, roll the dough up into a sausage shape. Cut it into 12 equal-sized slices and place them side by side on the baking sheet with the spiral facing up towards you. Cover with a tea towel and leave to prove for 45 minutes.

Preheat the oven to 200°C (400°F/Gas 6). Beat the remaining egg and yolk in a bowl and brush over the bun tops. Sprinkle with the poppy seeds. Bake for 10 minutes, then lower the temperature to 180°C (350°F/Gas 4) and cook for a further 20 minutes.

MUESLI BREAD
with Almond Butter

450 g (1 lb/scant 3⅔ cups) plain (all-purpose) flour, plus extra for dusting

60 g (2 oz/generous ⅓ cup) wholemeal flour

½ tablespoon salt

¾ tablespoon fast-action yeast

360 ml (12½ fl oz) warm water

oil for greasing

50 g (2 oz) pumpkin seeds

50 g (2 oz) almonds, with skins on

25 g (1 oz) raisins

25 g (1 oz) dried cranberries

FOR THE ALMOND BUTTER

300 g (10½ oz) almonds, roasted, with skin on

1–2 tablespoons groundnut oil

On a lazy Sunday morning, in your PJs and bed hair, this is the type of bread you want to be opening the oven door for. Slather in copious amounts of almond butter and jam.

To make the loaf, combine the flours with the salt and yeast in a large bowl. Pour over the warm water and stir till combined using a spoon or your hands. Lift the dough out and lightly oil the bowl. Put the dough back in the bowl, cover with a tea towel (kitchen towel) and let it rise in the fridge for 2 hours.

Remove from the fridge and add the pumpkin seeds, almonds, raisins and cranberries, and knead until just combined, keeping the nuts and fruits inside the dough.

Shape the dough into a smooth ball and put it on baking parchment on a baking tray. Sift a light layer of flour over the top to help it stay moist. Rest for between 45 minutes to 1 hour – the dough will naturally spread out into a round loaf shape.

Preheat the oven to 230°C (445°F/Gas 8). Pour 360 ml (12½ fl oz) of water into a high-sided roasting tin and put it on the bottom shelf of the oven. This will give the dough that lovely brown bakery-bought look, I promise.

Slash the top of the dough with a sharp knife, making 5 mm (¼ in) deep cuts. Put the bread in the middle of the oven and bake for 25–35 minutes until a deep golden brown. Remove from the oven and cool the bread on a rack. You can also take out the roasting tin now.

To make the almond butter, blend the almonds in a food processor. Scrape the sides down using a spatula and blend again till really smooth. Transfer to a small bowl or jar and top with the oil. This is ready to use straight away.

PUMPKIN BREAD
with Pecans & Chocolate Chips

MAKES 2 LOAVES

300 g (10½ oz) pumpkin

360 ml (12½ fl oz) vegetable oil, or any flavourless oil, plus extra for greasing

450 g (1 lb/scant 3⅔ cups) plain (all-purpose) flour

2 teaspoons ground cinnamon

1 teaspoon salt

1 teaspoon bicarbonate of soda

4 eggs

150 g (5 oz/⅔ tightly packed cup) soft brown sugar

150 g (5 oz/generous ⅔ cup) caster (superfine) sugar

150 g (5 oz) chocolate chips

100 g (3½ oz) pecans

This American-style bread is extremely soft, sweet and delicious, and slightly spiced with melted chocolate chips and crunchy pecans.

Peel and cube the pumpkin, then cook in a pan of boiling water for 5–10 minutes until soft. Drain and mash the pumpkin, then set aside to cool.

Preheat the oven to 180°C (350°F/Gas 4) and grease two 20 × 10 cm (8 × 4 in) loaf tins. In a large bowl, combine the flour, cinnamon, salt and bicarbonate of soda.

In another bowl beat together the eggs, sugars, pumpkin and oil. Stir this into the flour mixture and then fold in the chocolate chips and pecans. Divide the batter evenly between the 2 loaf tins and bake for 60–70 minutes until a toothpick comes out clean when inserted into the centre of the loaves.

Leave the loaves to cool in their tins for 10 minutes before removing them. Delicious served warm, or leave to cool fully on a wire rack.

THE BEST BERRY MUFFINS

MAKES 20 MUFFINS

350 g (12 oz) unsalted butter,
at room temperature,
plus extra for greasing

240 g (8½ oz) caster
(superfine) sugar

3 eggs

400 g (14 oz) plain
(all-purpose) flour

10 g (½ oz) baking powder

150 ml (5 fl oz) whole milk

2 handfuls of fresh or frozen
mixed berries

icing (confectioner's) sugar
to serve

This recipe was given to me – actually, I had to beg for it – from an excellent French chef. Once you've made the batter for the muffins, it can be kept in the fridge for up to 3 days if you don't want to make them all at once.

Preheat the oven to 180°C (350°F/Gas 4). In a large bowl, cream together the butter and sugar using electric beaters until pale and fluffy. Add the eggs one at a time to the mixture; if it looks like it is starting to split, mix in 1 tablespoon of the flour. Sift in the flour and baking powder and mix well to combine (you can use the electric beaters to do this if you want). Pour in the milk and combine.

Grease a muffin tin with some butter; if your tin gets used and abused as much as mine, you might need to sift a little flour into each buttered mould to stop the muffins from sticking. Spoon the mixture into each mould, filling them three quarters of the way full. Sprinkle about 3–4 berries into each mould and slightly press them into the mixture.

Bake in the oven for 25 minutes until they are lightly browned and cooked in the centre. Test they are cooked through by pushing a toothpick into a muffin and if it comes out clean, you know they are ready.

Let the muffins sit in the tin for a couple of minutes before transferring them to a cooling rack. Dust with icing sugar and serve.

BRAN, DATE & BANANA MUFFINS
with Salted Caramel Spread

MAKES 12 MUFFINS

butter for greasing

300 g (10½ oz) wheat bran

75 g (2½ oz) dried dates, chopped

75 g (2½ oz) mix of hazelnuts and almonds, chopped

75 g (2½ oz) plain (all-purpose) or wholemeal flour

1 teaspoon baking powder

1 teaspoon bicarbonate of soda

1 teaspoon ground cinnamon

240 ml (8½ fl oz) milk

175 ml (6 fl oz) golden syrup

1 egg

2 large overripe bananas, mashed

FOR THE SALTED CARAMEL SPREAD

300 g (10½ oz) golden granulated sugar

50 ml (2 fl oz) water

240 g (8½ oz) unsalted butter, cut into small chunks

¾ teaspoon sea salt

200 ml (7 fl oz) double (heavy) cream

This special recipe came from New Zealand and has been passed to me by my mum. She went travelling there one year and ate an array of bran muffins wherever she stayed. She's honed the recipe and here we have it. I couldn't help but add a little spread to go with it.

For the muffins, preheat the oven to 200°C (400°F/Gas 6) and grease a muffin tin with a little butter. Put the bran, dates and nuts into a large bowl. Sift over the flour, baking powder, bicarbonate of soda and cinnamon.

Pour the milk into a separate bowl and add the golden syrup, egg and mashed bananas, and lightly whisk together. Tip this into the dry ingredients and fold everything together just until the bran is evenly dampened – do not over mix.

Divide the mixture evenly into the muffin tin and bake in the oven for about 7 minutes, or until the muffins spring back when gently pressed in the middle. Leave for a few minutes before twisting and removing them from the pan.

To make the salted caramel spread, put the sugar and water in a saucepan over a low heat. Keep an eye on it and cook until it turns golden brown – no stirring is needed. Add the butter a little bit at a time while gently stirring with a wooden spoon. When all the butter has been incorporated, add the salt and cook for a further minute. Take off the heat and pour into a jar or ramekin to cool. Keep it in the fridge so it has a lovely spreadable consistency. The spread will last for 3 months if you store it in a sterilised jar with a lid on.

CLASSIC LEMON & POPPY SEED MUFFINS

MAKES 16 MUFFINS

100 g (3½ oz) unsalted butter, melted, plus extra for greasing

300 g (10½ oz) self-raising flour

280 g (10 oz) caster (superfine) sugar

1 teaspoon bicarbonate of soda

75 g (2½ oz) poppy seeds

2 lemons

2 large eggs

240 ml (8½ fl oz) whole milk

These are slightly crunchy round the outside and soft in the middle. Rising in the warm oven, these sweet lemony muffins might make a regular feature in your household like mine!

Grease a muffin tin with butter and preheat the oven to 200°C (400°F/Gas 6). Combine together the flour, 225 g (8 oz) of the sugar, the bicarbonate of soda, the poppy seeds and the grated zest of the lemons in a bowl.

In another bowl pour in the melted butter, eggs and milk, and beat with a fork until everything is thoroughly combined. Tip the egg mixture into the flour mixture and fold until all the flour is wet – do not beat it until it's smooth. Spoon the mixture into the muffin tin and bake for 10–15 minutes until risen and cooked through.

Juice the lemons into a bowl and mix with the remaining sugar. Brush this over the baked muffins.

SPICED GRANNY SMITH FRITTERS

MAKES ABOUT 20 FRITTERS

225 g (8 oz) self-raising flour

2 tablespoons caster (superfine) sugar

¼ teaspoon ground ginger

pinch of ground nutmeg

pinch of ground cloves

2 large granny smith apples, peeled and cut into 5 mm (¼ in) cubes

2 eggs, beaten

180 ml (6½ fl oz) whole milk

½ teaspoon vanilla extract

butter for frying

icing (confectioner's) sugar to serve

For those of you who love apples and doughnuts, these fritters are a delicious combination of the two – crispy on the outside with soft, tart apple in the middle.

I sometimes make a dipping sauce of cream cheese, cinnamon and honey to serve with these.

Combine the flour, sugar, ginger, nutmeg and cloves together in a bowl. Add the apple and toss around in the dry mixture until all the cubes are well coated. Pour in the eggs, milk and vanilla extract and stir gently until everything is combined.

Put a small knob of butter into a heavy-based frying pan over a medium heat. Use a large spoon to add a portion of apple batter to the pan. Spoon more fritters into the pan, but don't overcrowd it – I find doing 4–5 at a time is enough. Fry for 2–3 minutes until golden and then flip the fritters over to fry the other side for a further 2–3 minutes until golden and crisp all over. Remove the fritters from the pan using a slotted spoon or spatula and drain on kitchen towel (kitchen paper). Add more batter to the pan and continue cooking until all the batter is finished. You can crisp the fritters back up in a very hot oven for 5 minutes before serving.

BACON & EGG TOAST MUFFINS

MAKES 6 MUFFINS

3 tablespoons melted unsalted butter

6 medium slices white or brown bread

6 rashers (slices) smoked streaky bacon

4 spring onions (scallions), thinly sliced

6 eggs

salt and freshly ground black pepper

6 portobello mushrooms, grilled, to serve

vine tomatoes, roasted, to serve

This breakfast not only tastes great but looks really impressive, and it doesn't take much effort. I have used normal sliced white or brown bread for this recipe, but if you wanted to go all out you could use puff pastry or even corn tortillas for those who are wheat intolerant. I like mixing it up a bit by replacing the bacon with prosciutto and adding a few sun-dried tomatoes and slices of mozzarella.

I find that a standard muffin tin works well for this recipe, but you could use ramekins or even dariole moulds.

Preheat the oven to 190°C (375°F/Gas 5) and grease a muffin tin with the melted butter. Flatten the slices of bread by rolling over each one a few times with a rolling pin. Use a 10 cm (4¼ in) round biscuit cutter to cut a circle out of each slice of bread. If you don't have one of these, you can use a pair of kitchen scissors to cut out the circle instead. Cut one of the circles in half and push one half down into a mould in the muffin tin, with the curved edge at the top, so the edges of the bread stick up out of the mould. Then push the other half in the mould so that the two halves overlap slightly and completely line the mould. If you find you have some gaps, just use some of the bread you cut off to fill them in. Brush the bread with the remaining melted butter.

In a heavy-based frying pan, fry the bacon on one side over a medium heat for 4 minutes without flipping it over.

Lay a piece of bacon, cooked side down, into each muffin cup. Sprinkle some spring onion evenly over the bacon and then crack an egg into each muffin cup. Season and bake for 20 minutes in the oven.

Run a small knife around the bread, which will now be toasted, and pop out each muffin from the tin. Serve immediately with a large grilled mushroom and some roasted vine tomatoes to make a complete dish. Otherwise these are great on their own for elevenses.

CEREAL DATE FLAPJACKS

MAKES 16 FLAPJACKS

butter for greasing
225 g (8 oz) dried dates
175 g (6 oz) unsalted butter
3 tablespoons honey
75 g (2½ oz) soft brown sugar
½ teaspoon salt
300 g (10½ oz) rolled oats
1 tablespoon pumpkin seeds
1 tablespoon sesame seeds
1 tablespoon sunflower seeds

Need breakfast on the hoof? These are for you. Seed-packed goodness with a gooey date middle, these flapjacks will stave off any unwanted snacks you might be tempted by. You can also use apricots or prunes instead of dates if you prefer.

Preheat the oven to 190°C (375°F/Gas 5) and grease a 20 cm (8 in) square cake tin. Put the dates into a saucepan with a splash of water and heat for 5 minutes. Mash up the dates with the back of a fork and remove from the heat.

Melt the butter, honey, sugar and salt together in a large saucepan. Add the oats and seeds and mix until they are all fully coated with the butter mixture.

Spoon half of the mixture into the cake tin and press down to flatten. Spread the sticky date mixture evenly over the top and then cover the date layer with the rest of the oat mixture. Spread it out evenly and press down again.

Bake for 20–25 minutes until golden. Remove from the oven and score the flapjack into 16 squares using a small knife. This should help when you go to break them up once it has cooled. Turn it out of the tin on to a cooling rack.

Not only are breakfasts delightful eaten alone, they are just as special when shared. Sharing breakfast with a crowd of friends has a different kind of buzz to having dinner with them. Getting an invite round for a weekend breakfast seems to be a growing trend these days. So invite your friends round, along with any waifs and strays, and make them some of the following recipes.

FOR A CROWD

MINI CORN BREAKFAST BURRITOS

SERVES 8

1 tablespoon olive oil

250 g (9 oz) minced (ground) pork

1 garlic clove, grated

1 teaspoon ground cumin

1 teaspoon ground paprika

pinch of hot chilli powder

2 tomatoes, seeds removed and finely chopped

4 spring onions (scallions), finely sliced

salt and freshly ground black pepper

8 large corn tortillas

5 eggs

1 red chilli, finely diced

small knob unsalted butter

120 g (4 oz) Cheddar, grated

2 tablespoons chopped coriander (cilantro)

2 limes, cut into wedges, to serve

Kids love these, and adults secretly even more! Spice them up as much as you want by adding Tabasco sauce (hot pepper sauce) or dipping them in a sweet chilli sauce.

Preheat the oven to 80°C (175°F/Gas ¼). Heat the oil in a frying pan over a medium heat and fry the pork mince for 4–5 minutes, stirring occasionally. Add the garlic, cumin, paprika and chilli powder, and fry for another 3 minutes until the pork starts to crisp up. Add the tomatoes and spring onions, and cook for a further 2 minutes. Season and keep warm in an ovenproof dish in the oven.

Wrap the corn tortillas in foil and put them in the oven to warm up while you make the eggs. Whisk the eggs and chilli in a bowl and season. Add the butter to a separate frying pan over a very low heat and pour in the egg mixture. Let the eggs cook slowly for about 5 minutes, stirring gently when the eggs start to stick to the pan, until they are just scrambled.

Remove the tortillas from the oven and increase the heat to 180°C (350°F/Gas 4). To assemble the burritos, lay the tortillas out flat next to each other and spoon a line of the pork mixture down the middle of each one. Spoon the eggs on top of the pork and then sprinkle over the cheese and coriander. Roll up the first tortilla and put it on to a square of baking parchment. Roll the parchment tightly round the burrito by folding the top and bottom edges of the paper over first, and then wrapping the long edges over and round the burrito to create a parcel. Repeat this for all the tortillas. Put the burritos on a baking sheet and bake in the oven for 8 minutes. Remove from the oven, cut in half diagonally and serve immediately with a selection of sauces and the lime wedges.

If time is of the essence, you can make the burritos the night before. Once you have rolled them up in the baking parchment, instead of baking them put them in the fridge until you want to serve them. Preheat the oven to 180°C (350°F/Gas 4) and bake for 7–8 minutes.

VIETNAMESE BREAKFAST OMELETTE BAGUETTE

SERVES 8

3 carrots, peeled and cut into thin matchsticks

5 teaspoons cider vinegar

5 tablespoons caster (superfine) sugar, plus ½ teaspoon for the eggs

2 bird's eye chillies, sliced finely (optional)

3 tablespoons soy sauce (optional)

8 individual-sized or 2 large French baguettes

8 eggs

6 spring onions (scallions), finely sliced

salt and freshly ground black pepper

oil for frying

2 handfuls of bean sprouts (ensure they are labelled as safe to eat raw and buy them as fresh as possible)

100 g (3½ oz) sugar snap peas, thinly sliced

small bunch of coriander (cilantro)

After returning from a trip to Saigon, I couldn't get enough of the Vietnamese breakfast staple known as *banh mi*. Sold on every street corner with the vendor's special chilli sauce, this sandwich comes wrapped up and served with slices of cooked pork and pate, or with an omelette. A deliciously fresh and tangy breakfast in a warm baguette – I'm hooked. You can also use eight individual sub rolls instead of the baguettes if you prefer.

Pickle the carrots by adding them to a bowl along with the cider vinegar and 5 tablespoons of sugar. Stir and leave to rest for 15 minutes, then drain and set aside.

To make an optional spicy dressing for the filling, add the chillies and soy sauce to a bowl, and press down on the chillies with the back of a spoon to release their flavour. Set aside.

If you are using large baguettes, divide each one into 4 to make 8 pieces of baguette. Use your fingers to remove the bread from the middle of the baguettes; this allows you to get more of the filling inside and gives the sandwich a good crunch – a popular texture in Vietnamese cooking. Use the bread you've removed to make breadcrumbs for another recipe or go and feed some ducks.

Beat the eggs in a bowl and then stir in the spring onions, and the half teaspoon of sugar, and season. Heat a little oil in a frying pan and pour in a quarter of the egg mixture, rolling it around the pan so that it covers the bottom. Fry for 2–3 minutes until it is golden brown on the bottom and then flip it over and cook for further 2 minutes until golden on that side too. Slide the omelette out on to a plate or a sheet of greaseproof paper. Repeat this with the rest of the mixture to make 4 omelettes in total. Slice all the omelettes into strips.

To assemble the sandwiches, butter all the baguettes and then layer inside each baguette base some omelette, pickled carrot, bean sprouts and sugar snap peas. Sprinkle some coriander on top and spoon over some soy and chilli sauce, if using. Put the tops back on each base to close the sandwiches and serve.

REFRIED BEANS, FRIED EGG & CHILLI SALSA TACOS

8 eggs
bunch of coriander (cilantro), chopped
100 g (3½ oz) Cheddar, grated

FOR THE MINI TORTILLAS

350 g (12 oz) plain (all-purpose) flour, plus extra for dusting

2 tablespoons olive oil, plus extra for oiling

½ teaspoon salt

225 ml (8 fl oz) water

FOR THE CHILLI SAUCE

6 red chillies, seeds removed

3 tomatoes, skin and seeds removed

1 shallot, peeled

1 tablespoon lime juice

1 garlic clove, grated

FOR THE REFRIED BEANS

1 × 450 g (1 lb) can cooked pinto beans

1 tablespoon olive oil

½ onion, finely diced

1 teaspoon chipotle powder

salt and freshly ground black pepper

What can I say . . .? These are tasty circles of fiery joy! Enough to kick-start anyone into a good mood.

Make the tortillas by putting the flour and oil into a mixing bowl, and stir until the mixture becomes slightly coarse. Add the salt and water, and combine using a wooden spoon until the mixture turns into a ball of dough.

Flour a work surface and tip the dough out on to it. Flour your hands and knead for 4–5 minutes until the dough becomes elastic. Wrap the dough in some oiled cling film (plastic wrap) and leave it to rest somewhere warm for 30 minutes.

Preheat the oven to 80°C (175°F/Gas ¼). Remove the cling film and put the dough back on to a lightly floured work surface. Divide the dough into 16 equal pieces. Roll a piece into a ball then flatten it with the palm of your hand. Use a rolling pin to roll it out into a circle about 7.5–10 cm (3–4 in) in diameter and set this aside on a plate. Repeat with all the pieces of dough.

Heat a griddle pan over a medium heat and dry-fry the tortillas one at a time for 2–3 minutes on each side. Keep the cooked tortillas warm wrapped in foil in the oven.

To make the chilli sauce, put all the ingredients into a food processor and whizz until smooth. Pour into a saucepan and slowly simmer for 10 minutes until the sauce has thickened.

For the refried beans, drain and rinse the pinto beans then keep to one side. Add the oil to a frying pan over a medium heat and fry the onion for 3 minutes. Add the chipotle powder and beans and stir. Pour in enough water to cover the mixture, plus an extra 1 cm (½ in). Bring this to a simmer and cook until all the water has evaporated. Remove from the heat and mash the beans with the back of a fork until they are slightly mushy. Season to taste.

Heat some oil in a large frying pan and fry the eggs to your guests' liking. Spread each tortilla with some refried beans, top with a fried egg and the pour over the chilli sauce. Sprinkle with coriander and cheese and serve.

DIM SUM ROAST PORK BUNS

MAKES 16 BUNS

1 tablespoon olive oil, plus extra for greasing

300 g (10½ oz) unsmoked pancetta, cut into small cubes

6 spring onions (scallions), thinly sliced

2 tablespoons chilli sauce

1½ tablespoons caster (superfine) sugar

3 tablespoons light soy sauce

3 tablespoons oyster sauce

500 g (1 lb 2 oz) self-raising flour

400 ml (13 fl oz) semi-skimmed milk

pinch of salt

hoisin sauce to serve

I love these fluffy white buns for breakfast. They're very popular in Hong Kong, where you can stop off at a dim sum café and grab a bun for lunch. This is serious comfort food for the Chinese, and it's rather fun making your own. You can either use a steamer basket and wok to make these or simply a saucepan with a steamer on top.

Heat the oil in a frying pan on a medium high heat. Fry the pancetta for 3 minutes, stirring occasionally, until it starts to brown and crisp up. Add the spring onions and fry for another minute. Add the chilli sauce, sugar, soy sauce and oyster sauce, and simmer together for about 30 seconds. Tip everything into a bowl and set aside to cool completely – the pork is best added to the buns at room temperature.

Put the flour, milk and salt into a food processor and whizz until combined. If the mixture looks too sticky and doesn't come together to form a dough add a bit more flour a teaspoon at a time – you don't want to make it too dry either. Lightly flour a work surface and tip the dough out on to it. Roll the dough out into a thick (around 2.5 cm/1 in) sausage shape. Cut the sausage into 16 equal pieces and flatten each one with the palm of your hand into a circle about 1 cm (½ in) thick. Set them on to a plate after you flatten each piece.

Place 1 heaped teaspoon of the cooled pork mixture into the centre of a circle of dough. Fold the dough over the pork and pinch the tops closed. Place upside down (so the messy edges are underneath) into a double-layered, lightly-greased muffin case and then into a steamer basket. Repeat this for the rest of the circles; you should get about 8 in the basket at a time.

Fill a wok with 2 cm (¾ in) of boiling water and place the basket on top. Steam for around 10–15 minutes until the buns are fluffy and hot in the middle. Serve with hoisin sauce.

WAFFLES

SERVES 8–12

4 eggs, separated

300 ml (½ pint) whole milk

300 ml (½ pint) buttermilk

450 g (1 lb/scant 3⅔ cups) self-raising flour

4 teaspoons baking powder

¼ teaspoon salt

100 g (3½ oz) unsalted butter, melted and cooled, plus extra for frying

These irresistible toasted waffles are still so popular, you would never guess we have been eating them since the tenth century. Consumed across the globe, and particularly in Belgium where there are over a dozen varieties, they come topped with a plethora of flavours. I've only given a few of my favourites here.

Put 2 of the egg yolks into a large mixing bowl and pour in the milk and buttermilk. Whisk to combine. Sift in the flour, baking powder and salt, and whisk again to combine. In a separate bowl, whisk the egg whites to form stiff peaks and then fold them into the mixture. Pour in the butter and gently fold through. Do not over-stir as you don't want the waffles to become tough.

Put a heavy-based griddle pan on a high heat and add 1 teaspoon of butter. As soon as this has melted, pour 2 cm (¾ in) of the waffle batter into the pan and spread it around the pan evenly. Lower the heat and cook for about 6 minutes or until lightly golden on the bottom. Using a palette knife, flip the waffle over and cook for a further 6 minutes on the other side. If you want to crisp it up further, cook it for a bit longer on each side. Tip the waffle out of the pan on to a large plate and repeat until you have used up all the batter.

You can break up the waffles into smaller pieces to serve. Here is a selection of my favourite toppings:

★ Bacon and maple syrup

★ Belgian chocolate and banana

★ Sugared pecans

★ Salted caramel and whipped butter (To make whipped butter, let the butter come up to room temperature, then beat with an electric mixer until light and fluffy. Add 1 teaspoon of icing sugar for a little sweetness.)

GREEN EGGS

FOR THE PESTO

large bunch of basil, leaves only

3 garlic cloves, peeled

handful of pine nuts, toasted (see page 38)

120 g (4 oz) Parmesan, grated

2–3 tablespoons good-quality extra-virgin olive oil

FOR THE GREEN EGGS

12 rashers (slices) smoked streaky bacon

2 tablespoons white wine vinegar

6 large eggs

20 cherry tomatoes, finely diced

1 red onion, finely diced

½ teaspoon caster (superfine) sugar

1 tablespoon chopped mint (optional)

salt and freshly ground black pepper

3 avocados

juice of 1 lime

1 red chilli (seeds removed), finely diced

6 slices sourdough bread

smoked paprika to serve

This is a popular Antipodean breakfast, often served up at the weekend for breakfast or lunch. I have given you my pesto recipe here as it makes such a difference if you make it yourself.

Make the pesto by putting all the ingredients into a food processor and giving it a few pulses. I like my pesto with a bit of texture so I don't blend it too much and leave it quite chunky. Transfer to a bowl, season, and leave to one side.

Grill the bacon on a baking tray under a hot grill for 3 minutes on each side, or until it's cooked through and crisped to your liking.

Meanwhile, pour 5 cm (2 in) water into a large, high-sided frying pan and add 1 tablespoon of white wine vinegar. Carefully crack the eggs one at a time into the water, making sure there is a little space between each egg. Bring the water up to a rolling boil, then turn off the heat. The eggs can sit in the liquid to stay warm while you assemble the dish. If the eggs aren't quite cooked on top, spoon a bit of the hot water over them and this will cook the top.

Combine the cherry tomatoes, red onion, 1 tablespoon of white wine vinegar, the sugar and chopped mint, if using, in a bowl to make the salsa. Season to taste.

Halve the avocados and remove the stones. Scoop out the flesh into a bowl and add the lime juice and chilli. Mash everything together with the back of a fork to get your preferred texture – I like mine to retain chunks of avocado. The avocado browns quite quickly, so it's best to make this just before you serve the dish.

Toast the sourdough and then spread each slice with pesto and a healthy layer of mashed avocado. Add 2 rashers of bacon to each and, finally, top with an egg. Sprinkle a little hot paprika over the egg and serve with the tomato salsa.

TURKISH FLATBREAD
with Halloumi & Red Pepper Pesto

FOR THE DOUGH

500 g (1 lb 2 oz/4 cups)
strong white bread flour, plus
extra for dusting

1 teaspoon salt

1 level teaspoon dried fast-
action yeast

225 ml (8 fl oz) warm water

150 ml (5 fl oz) plain yoghurt

1 tablespoon olive oil, plus
extra for greasing

FOR THE FILLING

2 tablespoons hazelnuts,
toasted

6 roasted red peppers (roast
your own or buy a jar)

2 garlic cloves, grated

2 red chillies, seeds removed
and finely chopped

1 tablespoon chopped
fresh mint

1 teaspoon dried mint

1 teaspoon dried oregano

3 tablespoons olive oil

1 tablespoon lemon juice or
sherry vinegar

450 g (1 lb) halloumi, grated

This lovely flatbread is called *gözleme* in Turkey. It's a staple in northern Cyprus and Turkey. The salty cheese and the sweetness of the red pepper pesto make this savoury parcel a perfect handheld breakfast.

To make the dough, add the flour, salt and dried yeast to a mixing bowl. Make a well in the centre and pour in the water and yoghurt. Mix together with a spoon until everything is combined – it will be quite a wet mixture – and then cover with a tea towel (kitchen towel) and leave for 10 minutes. Give the dough another mix with the spoon, then oil your hands and work surface, and turn the dough out on to it. Knead for 3–4 minutes then return the dough to the bowl, cover again and leave for 1 hour.

It the meantime, make the pesto. Heat the oven to 180°C (350°F/ Gas 4). Spread the pine nuts on to a baking tray and roast them in the oven for 5 minutes. They will be whistling when you pull them out, with a golden brown shine to them.

Put the peppers with 1 tablespoon of water or juice from the jar into a food processor, along with the garlic, chillies, fresh and dried mints, and the oregano. Blend briefly to just combine everything then add the olive oil, lemon juice or vinegar and the roasted pine nuts. Pulse a few times until all the hazelnuts are roughly chopped – don't blend them too finely. Transfer the pesto to a bowl and season to taste.

Flour a work surface and tip the dough out on to it. Divide the dough into 8–10 even sized pieces. Roll out a piece of dough as flat as you can, like cardboard, into a circle roughly 23 cm (9 in) in diameter. Spread the pesto generously over one half of the circle and sprinkle some halloumi on top. Fold the other half over the filling and pinch the seams shut.

Cook them in a dry frying pan over a medium heat for around 4–5 minutes until they start to turn brown and blister. Turn over and cook on the other side for 2–3 minutes more. Transfer to a chopping board and slice into strips.

ALMOND CROISSANTS MADE EASY

SERVES 8

150 g (5 oz) unsalted butter, softened

75 g (2½ oz) icing (confectioner's) sugar

4 tablespoons plain (all-purpose) flour, plus extra for dusting

300 g (10½ oz) ground almonds

8 large croissants

100 g (3½ oz) flaked (slivered) almonds

I often choose this croissant when I am out for a breakfast coffee. I get slightly excited by the thought of it, and once I get it in my hands, thoughts run away to a dreamland of almond buttery marzipan.

Preheat the oven to 170°C (340°F/Gas 3½). Put the butter, sugar, flour and ground almonds in a food processor and whizz to combine.

Split the croissants in half lengthways using a bread knife but do not cut all the way through to the back — keeping the two halves joined will help the croissants to hold their shape. Spread the bottom half of each croissant with the almond paste but reserve 2 tablespoons for later.

Fold the tops back over the croissants to close them and put them on a baking tray. Spread the remaining almond paste on top of the croissants and sprinkle over the flaked almonds. Bake for 10 minutes. Remove from the oven and dust generously with icing sugar before serving.

SWEETCORN & RICOTTA FRITTERS
with Crispy Bacon & Avocado

SERVES 12

olive oil for frying

12 rashers (slices) smoked or unsmoked streaky bacon

3 cobs of corn, kernels removed (see page 68), or 1 × 335 g (11¾ oz) can sweetcorn, drained

1 small red onion, roughly chopped

120 g (4 oz) plain (all-purpose) flour

240 g (8½ oz) ricotta

1 teaspoon baking powder

2 eggs

salt and freshly ground black pepper

2 ripe avocados

juice of 2 limes

yoghurt and chilli sauce to serve (optional)

Fritters are a fantastic meal any time of the day, and these special ones from Down Under are particularly good. There is the sweet popping of corn in your mouth as you bite into each fritter, paired with the salty bacon and creamy freshness of the avocado. I usually make double the quantity so I have some spare to snack on. You can keep them for up to 3 days in the fridge. I tend to reheat them in the oven at 180°C (350°F/Gas 4) for around 5 minutes.

Preheat the oven to 120°C (250°F/Gas ¼). Add some oil to a large frying pan over a medium heat and fry the bacon till crispy. Transfer to an ovenproof dish, cover with foil, and put in the bottom of your oven to keep warm.

If using fresh corn kernels, cook in boiling water for 20 minutes until tender.

For the fritters, put half of the sweetcorn kernels, the red onion, flour, ricotta, baking powder, eggs and seasoning into the food processor. Blend until everything has combined. Scrape out into a large bowl, add the rest of the sweetcorn and stir in.

Heat 1 tablespoon of olive oil in a large frying pan, preferably non-stick, over a medium to high heat. When the oil is hot, spoon 2 heaped tablespoons of the mixture into the pan to make 1 fritter and fry for 1 minute on each side until golden all over. Remove from the pan using a slotted spoon or spatula and drain on some kitchen towel (kitchen paper). Repeat with the rest of the mixture and then put them on a baking tray into the oven to keep warm.

Halve the avocados and remove their stone. Using a large spoon, scoop out the flesh from each half and slice it into cubes. Drizzle with the lime juice and mash it up a little.

Serve the fritters with the bacon and avocado. I like mine with a dollop of yoghurt and some chilli sauce.

BOILED EGG
with Soldiers

Sometimes the boiled egg is overlooked and not seen as a substantial breakfast option for breakfast. Try your morning boiled egg with some of these soldier recipes and you'll see it in a whole new light. Boil your eggs according your preference, as instructed on page 9.

CHEESY, SMOKY, KIPPER SOLDIERS

SERVES 6

250 g (9 oz) smoked kipper fillet (or smoked haddock or pollock)

300 ml (½ pint) milk

75 g (2½ oz) butter

1 teaspoon plain (all-purpose) flour

2 teaspoons wholegrain mustard

80 g (3 oz) mature Cheddar, grated (or Parmesan for a stronger flavour)

salt and freshly ground black pepper

handful of chopped parsley

6 eggs

6 slices wholemeal bread

Put the fish in a saucepan with a lid and pour over the milk so it completely covers the fish. Put the lid on and bring to a simmer over a medium heat, then simmer for 3 minutes until the fish is opaque and cooked through. Keep the milk and remove the fish from the pan with a slotted spoon. Flake the fish on to a plate, discarding the bones and skin, and put to one side.

Make a roux by melting the butter in a separate saucepan over a medium heat. Stir in the flour and cook gently for 1 minute. Slowly add the poaching milk, stirring constantly, until all the milk has been incorporated and the sauce is thick and smooth. Cook for 30 seconds more then add the mustard, Cheddar and plenty of black pepper. Taste and add more salt if necessary – remember that the smoked fish already contains salt – then add the flaked fish and parsley.

Soft boil the eggs according to your preference (see page 9). Preheat the grill to medium. Toast the bread and then spread the fish mixture on to each slice and pop them under the grill for 5 minutes or until the sauce is bubbling and golden. Slice the toast into soldiers, sit down and dip into your egg.

SERVES 4

2 courgettes (zucchinis)

200 g (7 oz) plain
(all-purpose) flour

1 teaspoon smoked paprika

salt and freshly ground
black pepper

4 eggs

2 tablespoons milk

250 g (9 oz) panko
breadcrumbs

50 g (2 oz) Parmesan, grated
(optional)

olive oil

CRISPY COURGETTE SOLDIERS

Preheat the oven to 200°C (400°F/Gas 6) and line a baking sheet with baking parchment.

Trim the ends off the courgettes and halve them lengthways. Depending on how long you want your dippers, half them crosswise if needed, then slice them lengthways into strips to make the soldiers.

Combine the flour, paprika and seasoning in a large plastic freezer bag, add the courgettes and give the bag a shake to cover all the courgette slices.

Whisk 2 of the eggs and the milk together in a shallow dish. In a separate shallow dish mix the panko breadcrumbs and cheese together, if using. Otherwise, just put the breadcrumbs into the dish.

Using fingers or tongs, dip the courgette slices one at a time into the egg mixture, then into the breadcrumbs, and then place them on to the baking sheet. Use a pastry brush to lightly coat both sides of the slices with oil, or spray with oil if you have a can of olive-oil spray. Bake in the oven for 15–20 minutes until the coating is crispy and lightly browned. Make the 2 soft-boiled eggs according to the method on page 9 towards the end of the soldiers' cooking time.

SPICY POTATO SOLDIERS

SERVES 4

5 medium potatoes (King Edwards or any floury potato work best)

2 tablespoons olive oil

1 teaspoon smoked paprika

½ teaspoon chilli powder, or more to taste

salt and freshly ground black pepper

2 eggs

Preheat the oven to 200°C (400°F/Gas 6). Slice the potatoes in half – leave the skins on – and cut each half into to 3–4 wedges.

Combine the rest of the ingredients (apart from the eggs) together in a bowl and add the potato wedges. Mix the potatoes so they are all coated with the oil and spices.

Spread the wedges out on a baking tray skin side down and bake for 25 minutes until golden and crisp.

Soft boil the eggs towards the end of the wedges' cooking time, according to the method on page 9. Transfer the wedges to a plate and dunk away.

BUTTERMILK BLUEBERRY HOTCAKES
with Coffee Mascarpone

FOR THE COFFEE MASCARPONE

1 shot espresso or 1 teaspoon instant coffee mixed with 2 tablespoons hot water, cooled

125 g (4 oz) mascarpone

1 tablespoon icing (confectioner's) sugar

FOR THE HOTCAKES

225 g (8 oz) self-raising flour

1 teaspoon baking powder

good pinch of salt

2 tablespoons sugar

1 medium egg

225 ml (8 fl oz) buttermilk

30 g (1 oz) unsalted butter, melted

100 g (3½ oz) blueberries or raspberries

olive oil for frying

maple syrup to serve

These thick, delicious hotcakes are a popular weekend brunch recipe in my household, which then turns into afternoon tea... In fact, they work as a snack at any time of day – I have been known to jump in the car, mid-bite, with a reserve wrapped in kitchen towel! These are also great made with raspberries instead of blueberries.

Make the coffee mascarpone by mixing the espresso together with the cheese in a bowl. Stir in the icing sugar and mix until it is all combined. Set aside in the fridge.

For the hotcakes, sift the flour and baking powder into a bowl, then add the salt and sugar. In another mixing bowl, whisk together the egg, buttermilk and butter. Add the flour mixture and the blueberries to the egg mixture. Carefully stir the ingredients together until just combined – don't over-mix the batter as it is better to have a few lumps than to over-work everything.

Heat some oil in a non-stick frying pan over a medium heat. Put about 2 tablespoons of batter per cake into the pan and fry in batches for 3–4 minutes. Flip the cakes over and fry for a further 2–3 minutes until the cakes are golden brown.

Serve with a dollop of the coffee mascarpone and a drizzle of maple syrup for some extra sweetness.

The breakfast drink is extremely versatile. From a cold fresh juice to a milky smoothie, or a hot steaming tea to a cocktail. Drinks that you want to make you feel different, drinks that we crave, drinks that we drink any time of the day. Here are a few classics mixed up with a few unusual ones.

CUPS, MUGS OR GLASSES

MASALA CHAI TEA LATTE

MAKES 4 CUPS

500 ml (17 fl oz) milk

3 teaspoons sugar

1 thumb-sized piece of ginger, peeled and grated

3 cardamom pods, seeds only

3 tablespoons chai tea leaves (available online or in most Indian grocery stores)

This is a popular Indian tea with a delicious array of spices. This tea makes you feel re-energised and is delicious for dipping biscuits in to!

Put the milk, sugar, ginger and cardamom seeds into a saucepan over a low heat and slowly bring it up to the boil. Continue to boil for a good 20 minutes, stirring occasionally, keeping an eye on it to make sure it doesn't burn – turn down the heat if it looks like it might.

Add the tea leaves and stir them through the milk – you may find that the milk forms a skin, but just stir the tea leaves around to get rid of it. Boil for about 2–5 minutes more to infuse the milk with the tea leaves; you want a light tan colour.

Strain the tea into a jug and then pour this into 4 mugs or cups, whichever you prefer, and serve. I'm quite partial to a drinking tea from a mug, especially in the winter when you can wrap you cold hands around it. Try dunking in a bombolone (see page 93). A soft, fluffy bun can be nice too.

BLOODY CÆSAR

SERVES 1

30 ml (1 fl oz) vodka, very
cold, if possible

1 teaspoon celery salt

½ teaspoon freshly ground
black pepper

1 teaspoon Worcestershire
sauce

½ teaspoon Tabasco (hot
pepper) sauce

180 ml (6½ fl oz) tomato juice

150 ml (5 fl oz) clamato juice
(available online if you can't
find it in the shops)

½ lime

celery or gherkin to serve

A classic breakfast drink in Canada, commonly drunk after a heavy night. I tasted clamato juice – a blend of clam broth and tomato juice – for the first time in Toronto, Canada. It is a great ingredient as it gives you the saltiness you crave.

I have been known, in the summer time, to grab a punnet of really sweet cherry tomatoes to make fresh tomato juice for this drink. Just whizz them in a food processor and push the juice through a sieve into a jug or bowl. This gives the drink a lovely sweetness – far superior to the stuff out of a carton or bottle.

Put the bottle of vodka in the freezer for at least an hour before making this drink, if possible. Mix the celery salt and pepper together in a shallow dish. Wet the rim of a glass and dip it in the mixture to coat the rim of the glass. Fill the glass halfway with ice.

Pour the vodka, Worcestershire and Tabasco sauces, and tomato and clamato juices into a jug. Squeeze the lime juice on top. Give it a good stir and pour the cocktail into the prepared glass. Garnish with leafy celery or, if you are feeling daring, stick half a large gherkin in it.

If you want to make this for lots of people, you can make the mixer (the tomato and clamato juices with the Tabasco and Worcestershire sauces) a few days before, as the flavour gets better the longer you leave it. That then gives you time to remember to put the vodka in the freezer!

FIG & ALMOND MILKSHAKE

SERVES 2

225 g (8 oz) whole blanched almonds or 450 ml (16 fl oz) shop–bought almond milk

450 ml (16 fl oz) water, plus more for soaking

8–10 fresh, ripe figs

2 ripe bananas

1 tablespoon ground cinnamon

pinch of salt

1 tablespoon olive or flaxseed oil

Towards the end of the summer, when figs are plump and ripe and irresistible, I buy in abundance to make this special shake. Figs are an alkaline food, which is what we should be eating more of to balance our often acidic diet. Full of vitamins and minerals, and lots of dietary fibre, they're crammed full of goodness.

To make your own almond milk put the almonds in a bowl, cover them with water and then cover the bowl with cling film (plastic wrap). Leave to soak overnight or, ideally, for 2 nights – the longer you soak them, the more silky and mellow the flavour of the milk will be. Drain off the liquid and discard. Tip the soaked almonds into a blender and add the 450 ml (16 fl oz) water. Blend for 2 minutes continuously until you have a smooth mixture. If you are using a food processor, you may need to blend for a bit longer – up to 4 minutes. Once smooth, strain through a fine sieve into a bowl and discard the pulp in the sieve.

Pour the strained milk back into the blender or food processor. Wash the figs, then add them to the blender. Also add the bananas, cinnamon and salt. Blend for 30 seconds in a blender or for 1 minute in a food processor. Add the oil and pulse for a couple of seconds.

PEANUT BUTTER, BANANA & PUMPKIN SMOOTHIE

SERVES 4

200 g (7 oz) pumpkin,
peeled, chopped, roasted
and cooled

225 ml (8 fl oz) vanilla
yoghurt

8 ice cubes

2 tablespoons smooth
peanut butter

70 ml (2½ fl oz) fresh orange
juice

1 teaspoon vanilla extract

1 tablespoon soft light
brown sugar

¼ teaspoon ground nutmeg

½ teaspoon ground
cinnamon

1 ripe banana, peeled

This is the silkiest, smoothest drink you will ever taste.
Perfect for keeping in the fridge so you can go back for more
throughout the day.

Put all the ingredients into a blender and whizz for at least
30 seconds until perfectly smooth. Check the consistency; if
needed, pulse it a bit more. Pour into your favourite glass and sip
away. The smoothie can stay in the fridge for up to 3 days.

GREEN VIRGIN

SERVES 1

2 handfuls of rocket

25 g (1 oz) ginger, peeled

½ cucumber

1 apple, peeled and cored

1 green pepper, halved and
seeds removed

3 pickled green jalapeños
(feel free to adjust to your
own spice level)

mint leaves, to serve

This juice was accidentally created one morning when I had only a very few ingredients and I fancied something spicy. I have called it a Green Virgin as you could add vodka if you feel so inclined! A Green Mary . . .? Well, that just doesn't sound right. Or maybe it is Mary's antidote.

Place all the ingredients into a food processor with a dash of water. Blend for 30 seconds. If you like a more watery consistency, add more water and blend again. Strain the mixture through a sieve over a bowl; discard the pulp in the sieve. If you have a juicer, you can use this to juice all the ingredients instead.

Pour into a tall ice-filled glass and decorate with mint leaves or maybe just a slice of jalapeno if you prefer.

ICED COFFEE

SERVES 2

110 g (3¾ oz) ground coffee
2.3 litres (4 pints) water
ice cubes

A very popular drink and definitely one I like to have in the summer months. I've tried all sorts of ways to make it, but I find this way works best. If you double up the recipe you'll have enough to last you a whole month. For the best flavour use a strong, rich coffee to make this.

Put the coffee into a large container with a lid or a bowl that can fit in your fridge. Pour the water into the container and stir to mix in the coffee. Put the lid on, or cover with cling film (plastic wrap) if using a bowl, and leave it in the fridge for 8 hours.

Strain the coffee into a clean, large jug or bowl through a sieve lined with a coffee filter paper or a cheesecloth. Put some ice into a glass and pour over some coffee. Top with milk, to taste, and add sugar or a nutty syrup to sweeten to how you like it.

The coffee can stay in your fridge for up to 1 month, which means you can make iced coffee whenever you crave it.

REALLY CHOCOLATEY HOT CHOCOLATE

SERVES 4

900 ml (1 pint 11 fl oz) whole milk

150 g (5 oz) dark (bittersweet) chocolate (minimum 70% cocoa), grated

60 g (2 oz) milk chocolate, grated

150 ml (5 fl oz) single cream (half and half)

pinch of ground cinnamon

pinch of salt

Cold winter mornings equal woolly socks, polo necks and croissants dipped in hot chocolate. I like my hot chocolate dipped into. It reminds me of being in France, copying my French exchange friend; not really knowing how to do it at first and feeling a bit naughty, and very happy with discovering a new way of enjoying hot chocolate. This recipe is über-chocolatey, with a hint of cinnamon just to make it feel a little warmer in the mouth.

In a large saucepan, add 300 ml (½ pint) of the milk and put it on a medium heat. Once the milk is warm, stir in both chocolates. When these have melted, whisk in the rest of the milk and the cream. Bring the mixture back up to warm, but not boiling, and add the cinnamon and salt.

Serve in 4 large mugs.

INDEX

Page references in *italics* are illustrations

ACKNOWLEDGEMENTS

This has been such an enjoyable book to research and write, I wish to thank Kate, Kajal and Susan at Hardie Grant for making it happen. Danielle Wood, thank you for your fantastic photographs, you have been a brilliant person to work with. Nicky Barneby, thank you for your inspired design – you just got it from the very start, and have bought a real sense of style and originality to this book. I love it! Poppy Campbell, after receiving your only Brownie badge for making 'eggy bread', I don't think I could have had a better assistant on this shoot. Everyone who came and volunteered this summer in Italy, I would like to thank you for testing and tasting all the recipes, your comments have been most welcome.

My brother Marcus, thank you for allowing our endless chats on all things food. Mum and Malcolm thank you for your constant support and encouraging my continuous passion of food. A final thank you to Mr Green, Jono, my suffering partner who I love so much, thank you for putting up with my laborious questions, and my incessant breakfast banter. This would not have been made without you.

If anyone fancies a great place for breakfast in London, here I recommend my top three:

Dishoom

This places is inspired by an Indian style Bombay Café. Frenetic, exciting, and does the best sausage Naan sandwich and Chai Tea in town.

7 Boundary Street, London E2 7JE
www.dishoom.com

Caravan

Brunch at its best. Corn Morcilla Fritters with avocado. Try it, as you won't be disappointed.

11–13 Exmouth Market, London, EC1R 4QD
www.caravanonexmouth.co.uk

381

Old–style English café and fab for a fry–up, they let you build your own. Biggest Breakfast menu you have ever seen with lovely gingham tablecloths.

338 Bethnal Green Rd E2 0AG

Fern Green is a food stylist, writer, and boutique hotel owner. She regularly writes and styles for magazines and works with various high-profile brands on food styling for editorial, advertising and video content. She is also a recipe writer and tester and loves developing delicious new recipes to try out on her family and friends. During the summer months she cooks for her guests from her Italian kitchen garden at Fireflies and Figs, in Central Italy www.firefliesandfigs.co.uk

Breakfast by Fern Green

First published in 2015 by Hardie Grant Books

Hardie Grant Books (UK)
5th & 6th Floors
52–54 Southwark Street
London SE1 1UN
www.hardiegrant.co.uk

Hardie Grant Books (Australia)
Ground Floor, Building 1
658 Church Street
Melbourne, VIC 3121
www.hardiegrant.com.au

British Library Cataloguing-in-Publication Data. A catalogue record
for this book is available from the British Library.

ISBN 978-174270-915-4

Publisher: Kate Pollard
Senior Editor: Kajal Mistry
Cover and Internal Design: Nicky Barneby
Photographer: © Danielle Wood
Editor: Susan Pegg
Proofreader: Charlotte Coleman-Smith
Indexer: Cathy Heath
Colour Reproduction by p2d

Printed and bound in China by 1010

10 9 8 7 6 5 4 3 2 1

Find this book on **Cooked.**
cooked.co.uk
cooked.com.au